FAMILY Life ISSUES

Managing Finances

By David P. Anderson

CPH
SAINT LOUIS

Edited by Rodney L. Rathmann

Editorial assistant: Phoebe W. Wellman

Copyright © 1994 Concordia Publishing House
3558 S. Jefferson Avenue, St. Louis, MO 63118-3968
Manufactured in the United States of America

1 2 3 4 5 6 7 8 9 10   03 02 01 00 99 98 97 96 95 94

Contents

Introduction

▲ How to Use This Course

This course has been especially prepared for use in small group settings. It may, however, also be used as a self-study or in a traditional Sunday morning Bible class.

▲ Planning for a Small-Group Study

1. *Select a leader* for the course or a leader for the day. It will be the leader's responsibility to secure needed materials, to keep the discussion moving, and to help involve everyone.

2. *Emphasize sharing.* Your class will work best if the participants feel comfortable with one another and if all feel that their contributions to the class discussion are important and useful. Take the necessary time at the beginning of the course to get to know one another. You might share names, occupations, hobbies, etc. Share what you expect to gain from this course.

Invite participants to bring photos of their families to the first session to pass around as they introduce themselves and tell about the individual members of their families. Be open and accepting. Don't force anyone to speak. The course will be most helpful if participants willingly share deep feelings, problems, doubts, fears, and joys. That will require building an atmosphere of openness, trust, and caring between one another. Take time to build relationships among participants. That time will not be wasted.

3. *Help participants* apply the concepts included in each session. After each week's study, there is a suggested activity.

An old Chinese proverb summarizes the "why?" of the activity:

I hear and I forget;

I see and I remember;

I do and I understand.

The activity is to help participants do and thus understand. Encourage everyone to take time to do it.

4. *Encourage participants* to invite their friends—including their unchurched friends—to be a part of this study.

▲ As You Plan to Lead the Group

1. Read this guide in its entirety before you lead the first session.

2. Use the Leaders Notes found in the back of this guide.

3. Pray each day for those who join the group.

4. As you prepare for each session, study the Bible texts thoroughly. Work through the exercises for yourself. Depend on the Holy Spirit. Expect His presence; He will guide you and cause you to grow. God will not let His Word return empty (Isaiah 55:11) as you study it both individually and with the others in the group.

5. But do not expect the Spirit to do your work for you. Start early. Prepare well. As time permits, do additional reading about the topic.

6. Begin and end with prayer.

7. Begin and end on time. Punctuality is a courtesy to everyone and can be a factor that will encourage discussion.

8. Find ways to keep the session informal: Meet in casual surroundings. Arrange seating so participants can face one another. Ask volunteers to provide refreshments.

9. Keep the class moving. Limit your discussion to questions of interest to the participants. Be selective. You don't need to cover every question and every Bible verse.

10. Try to build one another up through your fellowship and study. You have your needs; other group members have theirs. Together you have a lot to gain.

11. Be sensitive to any participants who may have needs related to the specific problems discussed in this course, espe-

cially anyone who may need Christian counseling and professional help.

12. Be a "gatekeeper." That means you may need to shut the gate on one person while you open it for someone else. Try to involve everyone, especially those who hesitate to speak.

▲ If You Are Using This Study on Your Own

1. Each time you sit down to study a session, ask the Holy Spirit for guidance and counsel. Expect Him to work through His Word to encourage, motivate, and empower you to grow in your faith.

2. Study the Bible texts printed in the course with special care. God works through His Word. In it you will find power. Read each text slowly, several times.

3. Write answers in the spaces provided. Avoid the temptation just to "think" your responses. Writing will force you to be specific. It's in that specificity you are most likely to identify crucial issues for yourself. Check the Leaders Notes in the back of this guide for information you may find helpful as you go along.

4. Pray as you work. Ask God to show you what He wants you to see about Him, about yourself, and about your family situation.

God the Giver 1 ▼

Opening Prayer

Lord God, heavenly Father, how great and majestic You are! The heavens declare Your glory, and the skies proclaim the work of Your hands. Yet Lord, You chose to love and care for us. Our concerns weigh on Your heart. Thank You for Your goodness and love. Thanks especially for sending Your only Son, Jesus, as our Savior and friend. Bless us as we study Your Word. May Your Holy Spirit bring us new insights and a greater understanding of Your will for our lives. We pray in Jesus' name. Amen.

Focusing Our Attention

Some scientists suggest that there are as many stars in the universe as grains of sand on the earth. Yet our great and mighty God made them all (Genesis 1:16). As a young man, David, the writer of Psalm 19, had been a shepherd. When he wrote of nature proclaiming the glory of God, perhaps he was remembering quiet evenings when he sat on a hillside under the stars watching his sheep. There, in the majesty of a sea of stars, David wondered at the greatness of God.

Think of a time when you, like David, were moved to marvel at the greatness and majesty of God. Describe the time to a partner or to the others in your group, comparing it to one of the following.

1. an uplifting conversation with a friend
2. the birth of a child

3. the calm after a storm

4. the dedication and care of robins in the raising of their young

5. the beauty, color, and majesty of a mountain-view in autumn

Awesome in Majesty! Boundless in Love!

Although God may sometimes seem too great to be really close, the Bible teaches that He has come to be very near to us. He came in the person of Jesus Christ, and He came because He loved us. Knowing true love includes the willingness to sacrifice and realign priorities for the benefit of the loved one. God expressed His true love for us in the cross of Jesus Christ. By divine inspiration the apostle John wrote, *"This is love: not that we loved God, but that He loved us and sent His Son as an atoning sacrifice for our sins"* (1 John 4:10).

Christ Jesus shed His blood on the cross to win our freedom over sin, death, and the forces of evil that desire to maintain a hold over each human life. Tell how each of the following evidences pure, perfect, ideal love.

1. God desired an intimate relationship with us.

2. Jesus, the prince of heaven, left His throne to serve God perfectly in our place as a member of the kingdom He created and rules.

3. Jesus died so that we might live forever, taking our punishment upon Himself.

A God of Care and Promises

God is very great. He outshines the power and glory of the stars He created. Yet God is also very close to each individual person. He loves each person as if he or she were the only person He created. More splendid than a sea of stars, God's love streams from the cross where Jesus Christ died, from the tomb that could not contain Him, and from the day of Pentecost when He gave a special measure of the Holy Spirit to the members of His church.

God in Christ cares about our physical as well as spiritual needs. The material blessings He gives are always meant to benefit our spiritual welfare. Consider God's care over our lives in the words of Christ recorded in Matthew 6:25–33.

▼▼▼▼▼▼▼▼▼▼▼▼▼▼▼▼▼▼▼▼▼▼▼▼

"Therefore I tell you, do not worry about your life, what you will eat or drink; or about your body, what you will wear. Is not life more important than food, and the body more important than clothes? Look at the birds of the air; they do not sow or reap or store away in barns, and yet your heavenly Father feeds them. Are you not much more valuable than they? Who of you by worrying can add a single hour to his life?

"And why do you worry about clothes? See how the lilies of the field grow. They do not labor or spin. Yet I tell you that not even Solomon in all his splendor was dressed like one of these. If that is how God clothes the grass of the field, which is here today and tomorrow is thrown into the fire, will He not much more clothe you, O you of little faith? So do not worry, saying, 'What shall we eat?' or 'What shall we drink?' or 'What shall we wear?' For the pagans run after all these things, and your heavenly Father knows that you need them. But seek first His kingdom and His righteousness, and all these things will be given to you as well.

▲▲▲▲▲▲▲▲▲▲▲▲▲▲▲▲▲▲▲▲▲▲▲▲▲▲▲▲▲▲▲▲

1. Contrast the life God desires for His people with that of those who do not know Jesus as their Savior.

2. What promise does God provide for those who make spiritual concerns their foremost priority?

3. How can God's physical blessings to us benefit our spiritual welfare?

4. How might we share our physical blessings with others so that they might experience God's love in Christ?

A Changed Outlook

When God enters a person's life, He changes things. As His Spirit brings new strength and vitality, by faith He moves the people of God to honor Him, making the most of all they are and possess. Read Philippians 4:12–13 and summarize what Paul learned about getting the most out of life.

▼▼▼▼▼▼▼▼▼▼▼▼▼▼▼▼▼▼▼▼▼▼▼▼▼▼▼

I know what it is to be in need, and I know what it is to have plenty. I have learned the secret of being content in any and every situation, whether well fed or hungry, whether living in plenty or in want. I can do everything through Him who gives me strength.

▲▲▲▲▲▲▲▲▲▲▲▲▲▲▲▲▲▲▲▲▲▲▲▲▲▲▲▲

Consider Tom.

Tom was a hard worker. He worked 8–10 hours every day to pay his mortgage payment, car loan, and credit-card debts. On weekends Tom spent most of his time doing repairs on the house or his vehicles, and then there was the constant yard maintenance. When he decided to buy a new boat, he took on a part-time job that took up at least four evenings a week. In Tom's garage were a snowmobile, motorcycle, jet ski, and an antique Ford. Tom had lots of recreational options, but little or no time to take advantage of them. Tom and his family seldom had time to go to worship or do anything else together.

1. What evidence do you find of Tom's search for contentment? How does Tom's search compare with your own?

2. Pretend for a moment you are Tom. Apply the words of each of the following to yourself as you look for a way out of your dilemma.

13

▼

a. Since, then, you have been raised with Christ, set your hearts on things above, where Christ is seated at the right hand of God. Set your minds on things above, not on earthly things (Colossians 3:1–2).

b. Therefore, I urge you, brothers, in view of God's mercy, to offer your bodies as living sacrifices, holy and pleasing to God—this is your spiritual act of worship. Do not conform any longer to the pattern of this world, but be transformed by the renewing of your mind. Then you will be able to test and approve what God's will is—His good, pleasing and perfect will (Romans 12:1–2).

We all must admit that sometimes we worship the created rather than the Creator. Like Tom, at times we may be caught in a dilemma that seems to have no solution. Telling ourselves "set your heart on Christ not on earthly things" is often easier said than done. God knows that the things of this world will try to pull us away from Him. That is the reason He sent Jesus to the cross. Jesus' love for us not only motivates us to share His love for others. It also enables and empowers us to set our hearts and minds "on things above" to conform with God's will.

Gospel and Goods

The Good News of Jesus reveals God's invisible nature in a very visible way. It shares the love of God through Calvary and the open tomb. It changes hearts. Changed hearts continue to live in the world, but they are not *of* the world. Jesus sets us free to enjoy all of God's gifts to us without guilt and fills us with zest and thanksgiving. By God's grace, those who belong to Him can be the freest of all people, possessing all things necessary for life and held captive by nothing.

This Christian freedom was given to Mary. At the age of 78 she could no longer live in her house—a house surrounded by a white picket fence and lush beds of red and yellow roses that had been her home for 42 years. As she considered leaving it, she told her daughter, "God has given me this home for many, many years. I have seen most of my children go from diapers to wearing corsages to their high school prom. Within these walls I have celebrated birthdays and the sacred days of our faith as Christians. I thank God for all the benefits that have come to me in this house.

"I must leave it now, but I take all my memories with me. I look forward to what God has prepared for me in my future. Instead of growing roses, God may allow me to help grow faith in Christ among those people who will live with me at the Bethany Retirement Home. Someday, God will show me my true home in heaven. I am so grateful for all His mercies in my past, and I thank Him even now for the blessings He is yet to show me."

1. Describe Mary's attitude as she prepares to live at the retirement home.

2. How does Mary's attitude fit with the inspired words of St. Paul in Colossians 3:1–2 printed in the previous section?

To Do at Home

1. Take time as a family to look together at the stars on a clear night. Talk about God and His goodness to your family in Christ Jesus. Then pray together, thanking the Maker and Ruler of the vast universe for His love and care for us.

2. As a family, make a list of all the individuals, gifts, and possessions for which you are thankful. Set aside a period of time in which to thank and praise God for these things and ask Him to help you to use these things in ways pleasing to Him.

Closing Prayer

Think of one important insight God has given you in your study of this lesson. Thank God for all He has given you through Christ Jesus and for the help and insights He continually provides as you live your life for Him. Invite His Holy Spirit to go with you as you apply His Word to your life. Conclude in Jesus' name.

Making the Most Out of Me and My Possessions

2

Opening Prayer

Dear God, we confess that our lives aren't what they could be. Often we have failed to make the most of ourselves and the resources You have graciously given us. Forgive us, Lord, for Jesus' sake. Send us Your Holy Spirit so that we may make the most of all we are and have to Your glory and for the benefit of all whose lives we touch. In Jesus' name we pray. Amen.

Focusing Our Attention

Imagine you could choose to be any of the following persons described below. Share with a partner or those in your small group whom you would choose to be. Explain your choice.

a multimillionaire

a world-renowned personality

a brilliant medical scientist

an adventure-seeking world traveler

a powerful national leader

Looking at the Inside

You are invited to the home of a new neighbor who has just moved to America from overseas. As the coffee is being served, your friend sets a tray of chocolate candies in front of you. The candy looks interesting, and so you ask what kind of candy it is. To your shock, you discover that the candy is chocolate-covered ants. The chocolate on the outside makes the candy look good, but what lies on the inside you find disgusting.

Each person has a hidden problem that causes all kinds of bad symptoms. Since our first parents, Adam and Eve, fell into sin, we are born sinful. Martin Luther called sin *a heart turned in upon itself.* Our sinful human nature causes us to be primarily concerned about our own happiness, rights, and desires.

It promotes only self-serving usage of our time, treasures, and talents.

Our selfish natural inclinations can darken, distress, and even destroy our relationships—including those that are most important to us. Even within the closest of all human relationships, there emerges the need to assert one's own desires, pursue one's own felt needs, protect one's own territory.

But each person, Christian and unbeliever alike, also naturally possesses something designed to keep our selfish human nature in check. In his letter to the believers at Rome, the apostle Paul wrote by inspiration that God has also given unbelievers His Law to be present and active within them. Paul records, "... they show that the requirements of the law are written on their hearts, their consciences also bearing witness, and their thoughts now accusing, now even defending them" (Romans 2:15).

1. Based on Romans 2:15, why do those without saving faith sometimes appear to live moral, upright lives?

2. Comment on what each of the following Bible passages say about the ability of anyone, on his or her own, to make himself or herself free of the problem of sin.

a. The sinful mind is hostile to God. It does not submit to God's law, nor can it do so (Romans 8:7).

b. For whoever keeps the whole law and yet stumbles at just one point is guilty of breaking all of it (James 2:10).

3. The Good News for us is that God sent His Son to free us from sin and its hold on us. According to the following passages, how did Christ accomplish our freedom for us?

a. For just as through the disobedience of the one man the many were made sinners, so also through the obedience of the one man the many will be made righteous (Romans 5:19).

b. He Himself bore our sins in His body on the tree, so that we might die to sins and live for righteousness; by His wounds you have been healed (1 Peter 2:24).

Changed from Inside Out

When Jesus enters our lives, He gives us new goals and a new set of priorities. No longer does the selfishness that controls us need to dominate. With our best interest always at heart, His Spirit helps us to dedicate ourselves and our possessions to the service of God and others.

The change Christ brings makes His followers truly free. Instead of finding our sense of security and satisfaction in our house, our car, our clothing, our occupation, or our family, we can depend upon Christ, and He will never fail us. As the Holy Spirit strengthens our faith through God's Word as it is read, studied, and received together with the bread and wine in the Lord's Supper, He gives us a new sense of power over our circumstances.

Relate each of the following Bible passages to the place of material possessions in the life of a believer.

1. Give me neither poverty nor riches, but give me only my daily bread. Otherwise, I may have too much and disown You and say, "Who is the LORD?" Or I may become poor and steal, and so dishonor the name of my God (Proverbs 30:8–9).

2. But if we have food and clothing, we will be content with that. People who want to get rich fall into temptation and a trap and into many foolish and harmful desires that plunge men into ruin and destruction. For the love of money is a root of all kinds of evil. Some people, eager for money, have wandered from the faith and pierced themselves with many griefs (1 Timothy 6:8–10).

3. Keep your lives free from the love of money and be content with what you have, because God has said, "Never will I leave you; never will I forsake you" (Hebrews 13:5).

4. Put on the new self, which is being renewed in knowledge in the image of its Creator (Colossians 3:10).

God Makes Us Rich

God, the giver of all good things, will always equip us with what we need to serve Him according to His will for our lives. Whether He has given us great or little by way of material blessings, He wants us always to remain close to Him. Comment on each of the following statements in light what you know about God and His will for you with regard to your life and things He has given you.

1. Katie Luther often chided her husband for his generosity. Once when she called him to task for giving someone in need an item that had been given them at their wedding, Luther is said to have remarked, "God is rich; He will give us more."

2. "I am poor in material things, but God has made me rich in everything else."

3. You do not have, because you do not ask God (James 4:2).

4. Many possessions mean many responsibilities.

5. Charity begins at home.

Put to New Use

As God's Spirit changes families, He gives them the power and desire to use all that He has given them to His glory. Consider each of the following items. With a partner or with others in a small group, list three ways families can *dedicate* the following to honor Him, to share the Good News of Jesus, and to spread God's love as we serve Him and others.
1. a house
2. a car
3. money
4. recreational vehicles
5. children's toys

To Do at Home

1. Set aside a time each day as a family to talk about how each of you will use one or more of God's gifts to give Him glory during the days ahead. Pray together for God's continued blessings and for the motivation and ability to use them wisely.

2. As a family project, glue alphabet noodles onto a slice of dry bread to spell out "Give Us This Day Our Daily Bread." Coat with varnish and display in a prominent place to remind your family of God's goodness to you.

3. Tell your children how God has blessed you in both lean and plentiful times. Encourage your children to share their aspirations with you. Pray together that God will guide and direct them and continue to provide for them throughout their lives.

Closing Prayer

Lord of glory, You have bought us
  With Your lifeblood as the price,
Never grudging for the lost ones
  That tremendous sacrifice;
And with that have freely given
  Blessings countless as the sand
To th' unthankful and the evil
  With Your own unsparing hand.

Grant us hearts, dear Lord, to give You
  Gladly, freely of Your own.
With the sunshine of Your goodness
  Melt our thankless hearts of stone
Till our cold and selfish natures,
  Warmed by You, at length believe
That more happy and more blessed
  'Tis to give than to receive.

3

Living and Giving

Opening Prayer

Heavenly Father, You have given us Your best. Your only Son, Jesus, lived, died, and rose again for us. Help us always to give our best to You in our lives, in our relationships with our family and others, and in our use of Your many gifts to us. We pray in the mighty name of Jesus. Amen.

Focusing Our Attention

Choose the phrase from the following that best describes your attitude toward financial planning. Share your choice with a partner or with the others in your group.

1. Hello again.

2. See you later.

3. Do I have to?

4. Oh, no, not again!

5. Right on, according to plan.

We Are Stewards

Jesus gave it all for us. He came to earth and overcame every challenge and temptation, and lived a perfect, obedient life in our place. Finally He suffered a cruel death to pay the penalty our sins deserved. His resurrection victory brought us the assurance of a new and eternal life in Him.

Just as Jesus gave it all for us, He empowers us to live it all for Him. Not only does His Spirit give us the gift of faith, He also empowers us to act on that faith in our attitudes and decision making. God helps us to be good *stewards* of all He has given us.

1. By definition, a steward is one who manages the property and possessions of another. Since God gives all people all things, who are God's stewards?

2. Read the following verse from Hebrews.

And without faith it is impossible to please God, because anyone who comes to Him must believe that He exists and that He rewards those who earnestly seek Him (Hebrews 11:6).

What must someone possess in order to be a *good* steward?

3. Consider the following event from the life of Jesus.

▼▼▼▼▼▼▼▼▼▼▼▼▼▼▼▼▼▼▼▼▼▼▼▼▼▼▼

Jesus sat down opposite the place where the offerings were put and watched the crowd putting their money into the temple treasury. Many rich people threw in large amounts. But a poor widow came and put in two very small copper coins, worth only a fraction of a penny.

Calling His disciples to Him, Jesus said, "I tell you

▼

the truth, this poor widow has put more into the treasury than all the others. They all gave out of their wealth; but she, out of her poverty, put in everything—all she had to live on." (Mark 12:41–44)

▲▲▲▲▲▲▲▲▲▲▲▲▲▲▲▲▲▲▲▲▲▲▲▲▲▲▲▲▲▲▲

a. How did this women demonstrate her faith and gratitude to God?

b. Write a statement describing the widow's stewardship.

Finding Life's True Meaning

Like people today, the audiences Jesus taught were greatly concerned about matters of wealth and finance. Once a man in the crowd asked Jesus to settle an inheritance dispute. In reply He warned, "Watch out! Be on your guard against all kinds of greed; a man's life does not consist in the abundance of his possessions" (Luke 12:15).

Jesus then told the story of a rich man who focused his efforts on storing his abundant crop so that he could "eat, drink, and be merry" for the rest of his days only to be faced with his own untimely death (Luke 12:16–21). Jesus concluded the story pointing out that only in being rich toward God can one find true meaning in life. What do the following Bible verses tell about how we can be "rich toward God?"

1. Do you not know that your body is a temple of the Holy Spirit, who is in you, whom you have received from God? You are not your own; you were bought at a price. Therefore honor God with your body (1 Corinthians 6:19–20).

2. Command those who are rich in this present world not to be arrogant nor to put their hope in wealth, which is so uncertain, but to put their hope in God, who richly provides us with everything for our enjoyment. Command them to do good, to be rich in good deeds, and to be generous and willing to share. In this way they will lay up treasure for themselves as a firm foundation for the coming age, so that they may take hold of the life that is truly life (1 Timothy 6:17–19).

3. "Love the Lord your God with all your heart and with all your soul and with all your mind and with all your strength. . . . Love your neighbor as yourself" (Mark 12:30–31).

4. Whatever you do, work at it with all your heart, as working for the Lord, not for men, since you know that you will receive an inheritance from the Lord as a reward. It is the Lord Christ you are serving (Colossians 3:23–24).

5. If they obey and serve Him, they will spend the rest of their days in prosperity and their years in contentment (Job 36:11).

Rich toward God

As God's Spirit brings and keeps us in the saving faith, He moves us to honor Him with all we are, have, and decide—a response of total stewardship. Through the ages God's people have honored Him with a tithe, regularly returning to God a portion— usually 10% of the wealth they have received from Him. In addition they brought additional offerings of thanks to God at special events and occasions. God promises further blessings to those who, in faith, return to a portion of what He has given to them.

1. The people to whom God's Word was originally given were primarily those who worked the land. Consider each of the following passages from God's Word pertaining to tithes and offerings. After each, apply God's promise to God's people living today.

a. Honor the LORD with your wealth, with the firstfruits of all your crops; then your barns will be filled to overflowing, and your vats will brim over with new wine (Proverbs 3:9–10).

b. Bring the whole tithe into the storehouse, that there may be food in My house. Test Me in this," says the LORD Almighty, "and see if I will not throw open the floodgates of heaven and pour out so much blessing that you will not have room enough for it. I will prevent pests from devouring your crops, and the vines in your fields will not cast their fruit," says the LORD Almighty. "Then all the nations will call you blessed, for yours will be a delightful land," says the LORD Almighty (Malachi 3:10–12).

c. Remember this: Whoever sows sparingly will also reap sparingly, and whoever sows generously will also reap generously. Each man should give what he has decided in his heart to give, not reluctantly or under compulsion, for God loves a cheerful giver. And God is able to make all grace abound to you, so that in all things at all times, having all that you need, you will abound in every good work (2 Corinthians 9:6–8).

2. By God's grace, Stan and Carol came to faith after hearing the Good News of Jesus. They wanted to serve God totally in their lives, but their debt in excess of $60,000 troubled them. After praying for God's guidance and direction, they agreed upon a plan. Stan and Carol pledged to give 10% to the Lord off the top of their income. They decided to live within a conservative budget and divided the remainder of their income among their creditors each month. When the smallest of their debts had been paid, they thanked God and divided the money they had been paying that creditor among the others. Continuing in like fashion, Stan and Carol celebrated when two years later they found themselves completely out of debt.

Paul once wrote to the believers at Corinth, "The foolishness of God is wiser than man's wisdom, and the weakness of God is stronger than man's strength" (1 Corinthians 1:25). Explain Paul's words in light of the God's promises and the true life experience of Stan and Carol.

3. Look for insight in each of the following examples for your personal stewardship.

a. A member of the congregation's stewardship committee was received eagerly into the humble home of an elderly man who supported himself on a fixed income of $300.00 per month. Imagine the look on the committee member's face when the man decided to increase his monthly giving from $50 to $55 a month.

b. When Mandy and Mike were newlyweds, they reasoned, "We are just getting our finances put together and planning to purchase our first home, we can't afford to give much to the Lord now." When they reached middle age, they said, "We won't be able to give much now, we have to get our kids through school." Finally Mandy and Mike retired. They conclude, "We're living on a fixed income now, we sure don't dare to give much now. We have to keep a good nest egg for the unexpected."

c. "In Old Testament times a portion of the tithe went to do social ministry among the people, as taxes are meant to do today. So, I believe in calculating my tithe based on net rather than gross income," said Bill. "For example, a person's take-home pay of $1000 would place a monthly tithe at $100."

d. "Jesus Christ has done so much for us and we have always tithed and given to Him first from what we have," said Matt. "We have received far more than we could ever give. We have never had much by way of material things, but God has blessed us with health, happiness, and many good friends!"

To Do at Home

1. Discuss the saying, "You can't outgive the Lord." Together with your family, compare God's gifts to you with what you have given to God. Pray together thanking God for His generosity.

2. Assess your current giving. If you have not previously tithed your income, consider doing so in response to God's great love for you as a way of demonstrating to God that everything you are and own belongs to Him.

3. Help your children adopt the habit of regularly thanking God for His goodness by returning a portion of His gifts to them. Encourage them to tithe from their allowance or earnings.

Closing Prayer

Meditate upon the first stanza of "We Give You But Your Own":

We give You but Your own
In any gifts we bring;
All that we have is Yours alone,
A trust from You, our King.

After a few moments of silent prayer, join with the leader in the Lord's Prayer.

4

Managing Money God's Way

Opening Prayer

O God, how good and gracious You are toward us. Forgive us for Jesus' sake for our unfaithfulness to You in our attitudes and actions. May Your Spirit bring us to a greater knowledge and appreciation of You. May He renew, strengthen, and direct us in all our financial decisions. In Jesus' name. Amen.

Focusing Our Attention

Many of the psalms of David focus on the theme of the goodness of our loving and gracious God. Read Psalm 103:1–5 and list all the benefits from God that David proclaims within these five short verses.

▼▼▼▼▼▼▼▼▼▼▼▼▼▼▼▼▼▼▼▼▼▼▼▼▼▼

Praise the LORD, O my soul; all my inmost being, praise His holy name. Praise the LORD, O my soul, and forget not all His benefits—who forgives all your sins and heals all your diseases, who redeems your life from the pit and crowns you with love and compassion, who satisfies your desires with good things so that your youth is renewed like the eagle's. (Psalm 103:1–5)

▲▲▲▲▲▲▲▲▲▲▲▲▲▲▲▲▲▲▲▲▲▲▲▲▲

▼

Consider the item from the list for which you are most grateful today, and share your thoughts with a partner or with those in your group.

Getting Our Perspective

Through His Word, God helps us to recognize that the best gifts of God are spiritual. Material gifts do not endure and sometimes entice us into evil and become for us a curse rather than a blessing. Forgiveness of sins, a clear conscience, a giving heart, and a faithful outlook are numbered among the blessings God gives to those who trust in Jesus as their Savior. Our generous God has given the ultimate gift to us. He sent His only Son to be our Savior. Jesus went willingly to the cross, giving up His life to take the punishment we deserved because of our sins. With His resurrection victory, He proclaims to us the freedom to base and build every aspect of our lives upon Him and His unfailing love.

1. Apply each of the following verses to those, who by the power of the Holy Spirit, desire to honor God with the management of their financial blessings.

a. And we pray this in order that you may live a life worthy of the Lord and may please Him in every way: bearing fruit in every good work, growing in the knowledge of God (Colossians 1:10).

b. Make it your ambition to lead a quiet life, to mind your own business and to work with your hands, just as we told you, so that your daily life may

▼

win the respect of outsiders and so that you will not be dependent on anybody (1 Thessalonians 4:11–12).

2. The tragedies and brokenness of many of the world's wealthiest families prove the adage "money can't buy happiness." Still, many people act as though money is the most important thing in life. Even the people of God often center their prayers of request and thanksgiving around material blessings. Why do you suppose this is so?

3. Proverbs 24:27 advises, "Finish your outdoor work and get your fields ready; after that, build your house." Check any of the following items that adhere to the principle of this biblical proverb.

_____Placing completion of your education ahead of buying the house and car you have always wanted.

_____Taking a vacation instead of job-hunting after being laid off at work.

_____Buying a more expensive home than you can afford, trusting that you will receive a promotion down the road

_____Working to secure yourself financially before indulging in luxury items.

_____Placing your career before anything else.

4. Proverbs 22:7 states, "The rich rule over the poor, and the borrower is servant to the lender." God would have His children be dependent only upon Him, therefore He desires us to handle matters of debt responsibly in a way that honors Him. Below is a list of additional blessings that come to those who manage their debt well and to the glory of God, work-

ing to free themselves from obligations to creditors. Starting with number 1 as the most important, rank these benefits in their order of importance. Discuss your ordering with a partner or with the others in your group.

_____a clear conscience
_____character growth
_____no fear of legal actions
_____a good reputation
_____modeling of good financial principles for your children
_____a good credit rating
_____evidence of the Holy Spirit's guidance

5. Many states now sponsor legalized gambling through state lotteries. Furthermore, in some states gambling now ranks among the major industries in the state. But the gambling industry is based upon the fact that most of the time people lose. When could gambling threaten a Christian and his or her management of money?

Money Matters

As God's Spirit works in the lives of God's people, He guides and counsels us through the Word, strengthening, renewing, and enabling us to grow through the situations and challenges we face in life. Bill and Joannie, for example, had just begun tithing when they experienced a significant financial setback. After prayerful consideration and much discussion, they decided to continue giving to the Lord each month the amount they had pledged before their setback. During the months that followed, they often paused to thank God in silent wonder at how far their money went in spite of their reduction in income. "This past year has taught us to trust in God; He will always continue to provide," Joannie said.

Consider how God could build character growth in each of the following people through the financial situations they face.

Meet Sandy

Sandy's old car wasn't running poorly, but it was out of style. She prayed for a new car. One day when she spotted a newer car in the used car lot. Sandy thought her prayers were answered when she discovered that this car could be financed and covered within her monthly income. Sandy shrugged off her mother's advice that she not use up her entire savings on a down payment for a car but that she set aside some money for maintenance. Sandy *wanted that car* and made the purchase. After only three months of owning the newer car, the engine broke down, and Sandy had to borrow the money from her mother in order to get it repaired.

1. In light of Sandy's experience, how does a borrower become a servant to the lender?

2. As the Holy Spirit works in Sandy's life, what conclusion might she reach as the result of this experience?

▼

Meet Cindy and Dan

Cindy and Daniel finally decided to purchase their first home. After looking at several houses on the market, Daniel decided that they had found the one that was just right for them. Cindy liked the house, but felt that it was more than they could afford. To this Daniel replied, "It will cost us less than moving as our family grows, and besides, we're both sure to get raises."

At Daniel's insistence they bought the home of his dreams. As the months went by they made the bank payments and the occasional purchases required for maintaining their home. During the same time, they discovered they had less money to go out to dinner or take in a movie. Gas purchases for the car had to be watched, and avoidable trips were not taken. Cindy and Daniel began to have more arguments over little things, and found it difficult to agree on how to keep their budget afloat.

1. Most experts list money issues among the main causes of marital strife leading to divorce. Do you agree? Why or why not?

2. You are the trusted friend with whom Cindy and Daniel discuss their situation. What would you say to help them and to comfort them with the assurance of God's love and care?

Meet Mike

Mike enjoys the single life and the freedom of doing what he wants with his time and money. Mike especially likes the fact that if something costs more than his budget allows, he can still make the purchase using his credit card and spread out the payments over time. One day while paying bills, Mike discovered that the credit- and charge-card companies were wanting more in monthly installments than he could afford. Mike tried to find odd jobs to make up the financial shortfall, but couldn't get enough extra work to make up the difference. Soon he began getting calls from angry creditors.

1. How can credit card misuse lead to financial difficulties?

2. Comment on how credit cards may be used appropriately by a good "steward" of the resources God has provided.

To Do at Home

1. Set aside 10 minutes to talk individually with each of your children this week about giving—God's ultimate gift to us of His Son and our grateful

response to Him. Encourage your children in the tithing and wise management of their financial resources.

2. Make a list of the potentially dangerous threats in your financial management program. Ask for God's guidance and direction in managing your resources to His glory and your maximum benefit.

3. Finally, make a list from your check register or budget keeper of those expenses which you pay on a regular basis; for example, the monthly house payment. Bring this list to the next study session.

Closing Prayer

The leader will give each person a seed. As each of you hold the seed in your hand, think about one of God's blessings which He has allowed to grow within your life. Share your thoughts. Thank God for the blessings He will continue to provide for you in the future. Tape the seed in a prominent place as a reminder of God's goodness to you.

Living Stewardship

Opening Prayer

You are a great and awesome God, the giver of all things good. How generously You have given to us! Thank You for coming to earth as our Savior to always dwell among us. Help us to love You above all else as we live the faith we profess. By Your Spirit's power give us success in all we undertake to show our love to You. We pray in Jesus' name. Amen.

Focusing Our Attention

Share with a partner or with the others in your group which of the following grocery items best describe your approach toward budgeting and managing your finances.

Zest soap (Enthusiastic.)

pretzels (It puts you in knots.)

Mounds candy bar (When the pile of bills gets high enough, they get paid.)

potato chips (The chip off the old block—manage money like parents did.)

PayDay candy bar (Enjoy planning and following the plan.)

Quik drink mix (Get it over with in order to move on to something else.)

rubber bands (Usually stretched to the limit.)

God Is with Us

Immanuel, one of the names for Jesus, means *God with us.* As surely as Jesus lived, died, and rose again for us, He lives and empowers those who believe in Him as their Savior. Through times of prosperity and enjoyment as well as in times of want and disappointment, God continues to bless and care for His own. Consider the account of Joseph. Hated by his brothers, Joseph was sold into slavery.

▼▼▼▼▼▼▼▼▼▼▼▼▼▼▼▼▼▼▼▼▼▼▼▼

Now Joseph had been taken down to Egypt. Potiphar, an Egyptian who was one of Pharaoh's officials, the captain of the guard, bought him from the Ishmaelites who had taken him there.

The LORD was with Joseph and he prospered, and he lived in the house of his Egyptian master. When his master saw that the LORD was with him and that the LORD gave him success in everything he did, Joseph found favor in his eyes and became his attendant. Potiphar put him in charge of his household, and he entrusted to his care everything he owned. From the time he put him in charge of his household and of all that he owned, the LORD blessed the household of the Egyptian because of Joseph (Genesis 39:1–5).

▲▲▲▲▲▲▲▲▲▲▲▲▲▲▲▲▲▲▲▲▲▲▲▲

While Joseph faithfully served his master, he repeatedly ignored Potiphar's wife's attempts to seduce him. "How then could I do such a wicked thing and sin against God?" he reasoned. Finally, in order to punish Joseph for not yielding to her desires, she accused Joseph of trying to take advantage of her sexually and Potiphar sent him to prison.

▼▼▼▼▼▼▼▼▼▼▼▼▼▼▼▼▼▼▼▼▼▼▼▼▼▼▼▼

But while Joseph was there in the prison, the LORD was with him; he showed him kindness and granted him favor in the eyes of the prison warden. So the warden put Joseph in charge of all those held in the prison, and he was made responsible for all that was done there (Genesis 39:20–22).

▲▲▲▲▲▲▲▲▲▲▲▲▲▲▲▲▲▲▲▲▲▲▲▲▲▲▲▲

Eventually because of a special ability God had given to Joseph, Pharoah made him second-in-command of all Egypt.

1. Why did Joseph become a successful man?

2. How did the life of Joseph give witness to God?

3. When things turned sour for Joseph because of the false accusation of the captain's wife, did this mean God was not with Joseph? Discuss your answer.

Financial Planning

While the amount and type of blessings God provides may vary, God does provide each of us with enough material blessings to use to His honor and glory. As God's Spirit works faith through the Gospel,

▼

He raises in us the desire to manage our financial resources well as a thankful response to God for His goodness to us in Christ Jesus. With God's guidance and blessing, financial management can be an exciting and rewarding adventure.

Successful financial management begins with a plan or budget.

The purpose of a budget is to provide for optimal use of the financial resources to provide for the wants, needs, and security of the family. In developing a family budget, the entire family benefits when spouses approach the task, working together. Input and involvement from children also helps make budgeting and living within the budget a whole-family effort. Consider the following procedure as one way to set up a working family budget.

Using your figures, and the "best guess" method, complete Chart A, filling in the amount in the monthly column (if paid each month) or the yearly column (if paid out annually)—but use only one column for each item. You may choose not to write down the amounts, but to do a budget requires that you have a firm handle on the actual figures. You will also need to know your net monthly income so that you can compare it against your monthly expenses.

Ponder Points

As you look over your rough draft (Chart A), consider the following questions:

1. Does my contribution to church and charity reflect my desire to return "firstfruits" to the Lord and His work?

2. The finance industry uses some basic formulas to determine how much house a person or couple can afford. The first basic rule is that all debt (including all other loans, credit and charge cards, etc.), when added to the mortgage payment, real estate taxes, and home insurance, should be no more than 36% of

gross income. The principle and interest payment, taxes, and insurance on the home should add up to no more than 28% of gross income.

What is the percentage of my mortgage or rent payment to my total gross income?

3. Are my insurance coverages adequate—do I need more or less insurance, and am I budgeting for increases?

4. Am I setting aside enough money each month to handle the portion of the family's medical expenses for which I am responsible?

5. How do I budget for food and clothing for myself and family? Does the family prepare menus and purchase from prepared shopping lists (to restrain impulse purchases)?

6. Am I setting aside money for scheduled (new tires for the car) and unscheduled (car muffler blows out) maintenance required for the car(s) and house?

7. Am I anticipating (and setting aside money for) real estate taxes, federal taxes, state taxes, and social security taxes?

8. Am I reserving money for savings, investments, and for the family vacation?

Chart A

Budget Item	Monthly Payment	Yearly Payment	Monthly Income
1. Church Offering	_____	_____	_____
2. Other Charities	_____	_____	_____
3. Mortgage/Rent	_____	_____	_____
4. Gas/Electric	_____	_____	_____
5. Sewer/Water	_____	_____	_____
6. Home Insurance	_____	_____	_____
7. Health Insurance	_____	_____	_____
8. Life Insurance	_____	_____	_____
9. Medical Expense	_____	_____	_____
10. Food/Household	_____	_____	_____
11. Clothing	_____	_____	_____
12. Education Expense	_____	_____	_____
13. House Maintenance	_____	_____	_____
14. Car Maintenance	_____	_____	_____
15. Lawn & Garden Expense	_____	_____	_____
16. Savings Accounts	_____	_____	_____
17. Investments	_____	_____	_____
18. Personal	_____	_____	_____
19. Taxes	_____	_____	_____
20. Rest/Recreation/Relaxation	_____	_____	_____
21. Vacation Set-Aside	_____	_____	_____
22. Other	_____	_____	_____

Living Out the Plan

As you consider your monthly net income over against your monthly fixed and planned expenses, it may be necessary to make some changes. These changes can range from selling a vehicle in order to provide funds necessary to repay a loan to increasing the amount of money going into savings.

Once a plan has been adopted for bringing monthly expenses in line with monthly net income, a cash-flow system can be developed to monitor one's budget and better anticipate planned expenses. Purchase a ledger or make one out of note paper with pencil or pen. A computer spreadsheet program is also an excellent way to set up a cash-flow system. The cash flow should be for at least 14 months so that one can plan for inflation or changes within income levels due to raises, etc.

Down the left margin of the journal, list your monthly and yearly expenses. These items might be similar to those listed in Chart A. The column should include blanks for your actual spending each month. If you are using a fiscal year for planning your finances, start with January and list the months through February of the next year. When monthly headings and budget items are in place, use your "best guess" to fill in the amount you believe will be spent in each area during the period of your cash flow. Your sheet might resemble Chart B.

Chart B shows a sample family budget *before* it reflects any actual history. Note that the expense on some items was raised in January of the following year in anticipation of inflation or increased costs for goods or services. Monthly income was also raised in January on the basis of company policy which assured the family a raise in salary. A few of the accounts do not come due each month; the sewer/water bill, for example, is paid quarterly and the home-insurance payment is made only once each year (February). One helpful item, often forgotten, is the "Gift Purchase" account. Purchases for birthdays, anniversaries, and Christmas can heavily tax a budget and should be anticipated.

Certain items allow for you to move their unused funds forward into the next month. Clothing, Home Maintenance, Car Maintenance, Lawn & Garden Expense, personals, Gift Purchases, Recreation & Relaxation, and Vacation Set-Aside are all accounts that allow for unused portions to be moved into the following month. When a month is completed, actual expenses are plugged into each category and unused funds are moved forward in the appropriate accounts. The expenses are added up and compared against the Monthly Income—the remaining balance (positive or negative) is carried forward into the cash flow of the next month. After recording actual figures at the end of February and entering into March, your finance record would look like Chart C.

Remember that some accounts (Items 2, 11, 13, 14, 16, 19, 22, and 23 in Chart C) allow you to move the budgeted unused money within the same account to the next month and then deduct actual expenses, then move the remainder forward again. This allows you to anticipate a variety of expenses (new brakes for the car or the family vacation in July), or to save for such things as new clothing, all within the budget.

The "Personal" account is the money set aside as "mad money" for each member of the family. Some budgets will give an account to each member of the family in order to keep track of each person's spending. This procedure is especially helpful when some members choose not to spend their money during the month but bank it forward for a larger purchase in the future.

Chart C assumes that the family contributes financially to support a child in college. Savings is lower than ideal because of the money needed to go toward this child's education. Unlike this example, your budget may also show a line item for an auto loan. The above budget assumes that the car was paid

Chart B

Budget Item:	Jan.	Feb.	March		Dec.	Jan.
1. Church Contributions	300	300	300	<--->	300	330
2. Other Charities	15	15	15	<--->	25	15
3. Mortgage/Rent	600	600	600	<--->	600	600
4. Gas	55	55	50	<--->	50	57
5. Electric	40	40	40	<--->	40	40
6. Sewer/Water		150		<--->		150
7. Home Insurance		240		<--->		240
8. Medical Bills/Ins.	200	200	200	<--->	200	230
9. Life Insurance	120	120	120	<--->	120	120
10. Food/Household	625	625	625	<--->	625	640
11. Clothing	30	30	30	<--->	30	30
12. Education Exp.	300	300	300	<--->	300	350
13. House Maintenance	50	50	50	<--->	50	50
14. Car Maintenance	50	50	50	<--->	50	50
15. Car/Gas & Oil	125	125	125	<--->	125	125
16. Lawn & Garden	15	15	15	<--->	15	15
17. Savings Accounts	150	150	150	<--->	150	160
18. Investments	75	75	75	<--->	75	75
19. Personal	75	75	75	<--->	75	80
20. Taxes	150	150	150	<--->	150	160
21. Gift Purchases	45	25	30	<--->	300	25
22. Recreation/Relaxation	50	50	50	<--->	50	50
23. Vacation Set-Aside	75	75	75	<--->	75	75
24. Loans/Other:				<--->		
Total Monthly Income:	3,325	3,325	3,325	<--->	3,325	3,480
Total Monthly Expense:	3,145	3,515	3,125	<--->	3,405	3,667
Carry Over:	225	405	215	<--->	560	663
Monthly Cash Flow:	405	215	415	<--->	480	476

for before the child entered college and that other future purchases, such as new furniture, will be paid for out of savings. Note that the family received extra income in February because of an odd job done by the father. The money left over at the end of each month demonstrates cash flow and is carried over to do work within the next month's budget.

1. What other items would need to be included in your budget?

2. Why do you think that this family increased their donation to their church in February?

Benefiting from the Plan

As God continues to bless us through His Son, His Holy Spirit works through God's Word, nurturing, growing, and changing us into the people He would have us become. When God plays a major role in our financial planning and money management, our spiritual life benefits as a result. Brainstorm how God may bring you spiritual growth in each of the following situations:

1. Experiencing gradual success in working your way out of debt.

Chart C

Item:	Jan.	Feb.	March.	April	May
1. Church Contributions	300	315	300		
2. Misc. Charities	10	15	5		
3. Mortgage/Rent	600	600	600		
4. Gas	48	60	53		
5. Electric	37	42	41		
6. Sewer/Water		137			
7. Home Insurance		240			
8. Medical Bills/Ins.	175	240	190		
9. Life Insurance	120	120	120		
10. Food/Household	637	599	615		
11. Clothing		47	43		
12. Education Exp.	290	275	352		
13. House Maintenance			150		
14. Car Maintenance			70		
15. Car/Gas & Oil	95	1470	112		
16. Lawn & Garden			45		
17. Savings Accounts	125	125	125		
18. Investments	75	75	75		
19. Personal	42	108	26		
20. Taxes	150	150	150		
21. Gift Purchases	48	22	27		
22. Recreation/Relaxation	28	57	50		
23. Vacation Set-Aside			225		
24. Loans/Other:					
Total Monthly Income:	3,325	3,452	3,325		
Total Monthly Expense:	2,780	3,374			
Carry Over:	225	770			
Monthly Cash Flow:	770	848	848		

2. Facing financial ruin.

3. Overcoming addiction to gambling.

4. Tithing.

5. Looking for ways to use everything you have to the glory of God and for the welfare of others as a grateful response to Him.

To Do at Home

Put together or review your family budget. Pray together asking for God's guidance and direction in managing His gifts to you.

Closing Prayer

Take few moments to reflect silently on your family finances. Thank God for His many blessings. Ask Him to go with you and to equip and enable you in all the challenges and rewards awaiting you in the future. Conclude with the following.

Oh, that the Lord would guide my ways
To keep His statutes still!
Oh, that my God would grant me grace
To know and do His will!

Assist my soul, too apt to stray,
A stricter watch to keep;
If ever I forget Your way,
Restore Your wand'ring sheep.

Read **Ephesians 5:15–21** and discuss the importance to the kingdom's work that you practice wise Christian stewardship. How can good stewardship, along with music and song, be a thank offering to God? You may wish to close by singing the doxology.

Leaders Notes

Session 1

God the Giver

▲ Focus

Welcome everyone. Give each participant a copy of the Study Guide. Encourage participants to write their names on the front covers. Ask that they take the booklets home between sessions and bring them back each time the group meets.

▲ Objectives

That by the power of the Holy Spirit working through God's Word, the participants will

1. reflect on the awesome splendor, power, and love of our almighty God;

2. recognize contentment as a great gift of God;

3. express confident trust in the desire and power of God in Christ to renew and redirect the lives of those who belong to Him;

4. rediscover the sheer Gospel joy of giving ourselves and our possessions to God and His kingdom's work.

▲ Opening Prayer

Say, **Nature gives testimony to its Creator. The eye of faith sees the glory of a great God in His creation. The heart of faith understands that, as Author of all things, God is also the true Owner of all things.** Ask participants to join you in praying the prayer as printed in the Study Guide.

▲ Focusing Our Attention

Acquaint participants with one another by having them take turns introducing themselves and sharing something about their respective families. Begin by introducing yourself. Then comment, **David once wrote, "The heavens declare the glory of God; the skies proclaim the work of his hands"** (Psalm 19:1). Continue with the reading of the introductory paragraph in this section. Allow several minutes for participants to share with partners or in small groups about times when they too were moved to marvel at the greatness and majesty of God.

▲ Awesome in Majesty! Boundless in Love!

Read the material preceding the activity aloud to the group. Comment that God is far greater than our minds can begin to understand. Still, God has revealed Himself to us most completely in the person of Jesus who came to us as God's love in human flesh to live, die, and defeat death and evil for us. Invite volunteers to describe the pure, perfect, ideal love of God as evidenced in each statement in the numbered activity.

1. In spite of our sinfulness God refused to abandon us. Instead He continues to seek us in our lost condition. Desiring to be close to us, He sent His only Son to become one of us.

2. Jesus showed His love for us by willingly doing for us what we are unable to do by ourselves—love and serve God perfectly.

3. Jesus' love moved Him to place us first; He willingly laid down His life so that we might live.

▲ A God of Care and Promises

Have a volunteer read the introductory material in this section aloud to the group. Express joy and appreciation for the individual love, care, and concern the maker and ruler of the entire universe has for each person He has created. Have participants read the section from Matthew 6 and respond to the two discussion items in this section with partners or in small groups. Then review their responses as a whole group.

▼

1. Although unbelievers may be preoccupied with concern and worry over what they will eat and wear and how they will live, God's people need not worry knowing He will always love and provide for them.

2. God promises *all things* to those who by His Spirit's power allow God and the things of concern to Him to have top priority in their lives. Comment on Paul's affirmation of this same concept when he wrote, "He who did not spare His own Son, but gave Him up for us all—how will He not also, along with Him, graciously give us all things?" (Romans 8:32). Affirm spiritual concerns as of greater importance than those that are physical.

3. God works in our lives through His Word to bring us spiritual growth as we seek His help and direction in contending with issues and challenges involving our life's work and possessions.

4. Accept participant responses.

▲ A Changed Outlook

Say, **God wants people to get the most out of life. Jesus once said, "I have come that they may have life, and have it to the full"** (John 10:10). Read the opening portion of this section aloud to the whole group. Ask someone to summarize what Paul learned about getting the most out of life. Emphasize that God's people can possess the gift of contentment regardless of their circumstances.

Invite participants to work through the vignette and accompanying questions with partners or in small groups. Briefly comment about each discussion item as a whole group.

1. Tom is seeking his identity in the things he owns. His dilemma could be described in the words *possessed by possessions.*

2. a. God invites those who know the forgiveness and power of Christ to adopt an entirely new set of priorities, different from those of the world.

b. Comment that in addition to coming to us through His Son Jesus Christ, God has come and continues to come to us through His holy written Word—the Bible. Through His Word, His Holy Spirit helps us find and choose the choices God would have us make in our lives.

▲ Gospel and Goods

Invite a volunteer to read this section to the group. Underscore the freedom Christ brings to lives that could become weighed down by disappointments, obligations, and problems. Continue as a whole group with the discussion items.

1. Comment on the way Mary has learned to set her mind first on heavenly things.

2. By God's grace Mary can face her future boldly, with her mind set on things above, knowing that God will always care and provide for her in ways that will give her life meaning and purpose.

▲ To Do at Home

Encourage participants to do one or both of these activities during the coming week.

▲ Closing Prayer

Conclude this section as suggested in the Study Guide.

Session 2

Making the Most Out of Me and My Possessions

▲ Focus

Welcome everyone. Give each participant a copy of the Study Guide. Encourage participants to write their names on the front covers. Ask that they take the booklets home between sessions and bring them back each time the group meets.

▲ Objectives

That by the power of the Holy Spirit working through God's Word, the participants will

1. confess their sins of selfishness trusting in the forgiveness Jesus has earned for them through His life, death, and resurrection;

2. identify the change God brings to the lives of those who believe in Jesus as their Savior;

3. thank God for the marvelous ways He enables them to use His blessings to His glory and for their benefit and the benefit of others;

4. demonstrate a desire to dedicate to God all they are and possess.

▲ Opening Prayer

Pray the prayer printed in the Study Guide, or lead the group in an extemporaneous prayer.

▲ Focusing Our Attention

Use this activity to get the class off and running. Have participants share their choices with partners or in small groups.

▲ Looking at the Inside

You may want to purchase a small box of chocolate covered candy, the kind that has a variety of different fillings. Let each class member select a piece of candy and then try to guess the filling it contains. Continue by reading the information in this section. Comment that sometimes all of us feel like chocolate-covered ants. We may project an image of competency and togetherness while at the same time we are not at all pleased with ourselves for the disgusting ideas or thoughts we carry around inside.

Emphasize our natural inability to love and serve God as the result of our fallen condition. Have participants work through the questions with partners or in small groups. Then briefly review responses as a whole group.

1. All people—believers and unbelievers alike—possess the

law of God written on their hearts. The Law of God brings us to know right from wrong and to recognize the consequences of disobedience in our lives and in the world around us.

2. a. Because of our fallen condition, we are enemies of God. As such, we do not and indeed cannot keep God's Law.

b. Even those who consciously try to please God by their actions fall short and stand guilty and condemned in the eyes of God.

3. Emphasize the magnitude of the gift given on Calvary's mountain to cover the debt of all humanity's sinfulness.

a. Jesus came to be our substitute. He obeyed God in our place and God accepted His obedience and credited it to us.

b. Jesus paid the penalty we deserved, dying in our place to win forgiveness and eternal life and to defeat of the forces of evil for us.

▲ Changed from Inside Out

Invite one or two volunteers to read the paragraphs in this section to the group. Underscore the life-renewing, life-redirecting power of the Holy Spirit as He works in our lives through the Word and Sacrament. Give several minutes for participants to work with partners or in small groups to discuss the change Christ brings to His followers with respect to their material possessions. Reassemble the large group and invite brief comments on each passage.

1. God desires neither the abundance of possessions nor the lack of necessities to get in the way in our Father/child relationship with Him.

2. The love of wealth and the quest for increased financial gain can lead people to abandon the saving faith. But God desires to bring people contentment in knowing and living for Him.

3. God's promise never to leave or forsake us bears greater value than wealth or property.

4. As the Holy Spirit continues to work in our lives through the Word, God continually changes us into the people He would have us be with regard to our attitudes and actions—including those that involve our possessions and resources.

▲ God Makes Us Rich

Read the introductory paragraph to the group. Then allow participants to work with partners or in small groups to discuss the numbered items. After several minutes, briefly review responses as a whole group.

1. Luther's actions evidence a regard for possessions as God's gifts to be used to His glory and for the welfare and benefit of others as evidence of God's love in action.

2. In Christ, all who believe have inherited the greatest legacy anyone could ever possess—forgiveness, life, and salvation. God's greatest blessings are spiritual. The results of these are contentment, happiness, satisfaction, affirmation, etc.

3. God invites us to ask for material possessions. In keeping with other passages of Scripture, we know we also should pray that His will for us be done.

4. Since God always has our best interests at heart, we do well always to ask that God only gives us what we will be able to manage effectively to His glory.

5. Christian parents have the privilege and obligation of teaching their children in speech and by example a Christ-empowered management of all He has given to them. Invite participants to give specific examples.

▲ Put to New Use

Read the introductory material. Then invite participants to work with partners or in small groups to list three specific ways each of the numbered items might be used to honor God, share the Gospel, and spread God's love in ways that serve Him and others.

After several minutes have passed, call everyone back together for a brief recap of the ways suggested.

▲ To Do at Home

Encourage participants to do one or more of these activities during the week ahead.

▲ Closing Prayer

Join together in the reading or singing of the two stanzas of "Lord of Glory, You Have Brought Us" as your closing prayer.

Session 3

Living and Giving

▲ Focus

Welcome everyone. Give each participant a copy of the Study Guide. Encourage participants to write their names on the front covers. Ask that they take the booklets home between sessions and bring them back each time the group meets.

▲ Objectives

That by the power of the Holy Spirit working through God's Word, the participants will
1. explore the meaning of Christian stewardship;
2. recognize that as Christ has given Himself for them, He likewise empowers His people to honor Him with all they are and possess;
3. demonstrate a desire to return to God in thanksgiving a generous portion of His gifts to them.

▲ Opening Prayer

Show the class something from nature that shows beauty and complexity—perhaps a flower. Comment that just as God so carefully arranges the chemistry of this plant, He also guides and provides opportunities in the lives of His people. Invite participants to join you in praying the prayer printed in the Study Guide, or lead the group in an extemporaneous prayer thanking God for His goodness in Christ Jesus and asking the Holy Spirit's blessing upon your study of this lesson.

▲ Focusing Our Attention

Ask participants to do this activity, sharing with a partner or with two or three others in a small group.

▲ We Are Stewards

Read the opening paragraphs in this section aloud to the group. Underscore the great love of Jesus for us—a love that moved Him to live and die for our salvation. Comment that as Jesus calls us to be His own by faith, He gives us opportunities for joyful service in the new life He provides for us by the working of His Holy Spirit. Have participants work with partners or in small groups to complete this activity. Then reassemble everyone for a brief review of each item.

1. Since God gives all people all things, everyone is a steward. Each individual may be either a good steward or a poor steward.

2. Good stewards are those who respond to God *in faith,* gratefully and faithfully managing the possessions He has given us to use.

3. a. The widow gave to God everything she had to live on as a demonstration of her complete dependence upon Him.

b. Participant responses may vary somewhat. Affirm those that focus on the totality of the woman's stewardship. She gave all she had. Comment that the Spirit similarly moves believers to dedicate all we are and have to Him as a faith- and love-motivated response. Compare with a couple who, upon marriage, plans their life and future together, committing every possession and every aspect of themselves to one another, acting without force or obligation, motivated solely by their love one for the other.

▲ Finding Life's True Meaning

Invite a volunteer to read the two paragraphs preceding the activity to the group. If time permits, you may choose to read aloud to the group the entire account of the parable of the rich man as recorded in Luke 12:15–21. Continue with the discussion items.

1. We have been bought with a price. Jesus paid for us with His very life. Therefore, by faith we belong to Him. As the Holy Spirit works in us through the Gospel, He moves us

to honor God. We are rich toward God when our lives evidence His presence within us.

2. Those who are rich toward God, put their hope in Him, enjoying His gifts to us and willingly and generously using them to help and serve others. God promises that such actions lay up treasures in heaven for those who perform them in faith.

3. Total stewardship, as God's Spirit causes the motivation, desire, and direction to accomplish it to emerge within us, results in unselfish acts of love toward God and others.

4. Being rich toward God is first a matter of attitude. God brings His people to approach tasks and obligations with a wholehearted dedication and desire to succeed as a grateful response to our God who has given us everything.

5. Those who are rich toward God are motivated to seek His will and way in life and trust in Him to provide for them as He has promised.

▲ Rich toward God

Read the material in the opening paragraph aloud to the group. Explain the difference between a tithe and an offering. A tithe is a portion of income regularly allocated to God. An offering is a gift given to God over and above or exclusive of a tithe. Have participants work through the discussion items as partners or in small groups. Then briefly review responses as a whole group.

1. a. The Lord promises to bless those who thankfully acknowledge and respond to Him as Lord of their lives. Comment that the motivation for generous giving that honors God is a grateful response for all God has given us in Christ Jesus.

b. God promises to bless those who bring tithes and offerings to Him, inviting us to put His promise to the test. He describes blessings that go beyond material benefits.

c. God says that He loves a cheerful giver. He promises to bless His people abundantly so that they, in turn, may generously give to others to bring glory and honor to God as His kingdom is extended.

2. The experience of Stan and Carol illustrates that God keeps His promises. Many a household money manager can attest to how "everything works out" when God is honored with the "firstfruits" of the family income.

3. a. Giving is a Christian's joy and privilege. By the

working of the Holy Spirit, an attitude of stewardship takes hold in a believer so that he or she delights not in receiving, but rather in giving to God with a heart filled with love.

b. The experience of Mike and Mandy illustrates that there are always good reasons not to be a generous giver. By God's grace, the eyes of faith are enabled to see beyond these reasons to focus instead on the cross of Christ and the privilege of living as a child of God. For many, tithing involves sacrifice. It may mean that the family holds onto the old car for another year, or puts off the purchase of a recreational vehicle. What is as important in the giving is the spiritual growth of the family as they set their vision to a higher kingdom and purpose.

c. There is debate about whether the tithe should be figured on the gross or net family income. But whether an individual or family tithes on the gross or the net income is not as important as giving for the right reason. A wealthy person may give far more than a tithe, a struggling person may sacrifice deeply to give a tithe from his or her net income.

d. God's blessings always extend far beyond material things. His greatest blessings are intangible.

▲ To Do at Home

Encourage participants to do one or more of these activities during the week ahead.

▲ Closing Prayer

Conclude the session following the suggestion provided in the Study Guide.

Session 4

Managing Money God's Way

▲ Focus

Welcome everyone. Give each participant a copy of the Study Guide. Encourage participants to write their names on the front covers. Ask that they take the booklets home between sessions and bring them back for the final session.

▲ Objectives

That by the power of the Holy Spirit working through God's Word, the participants will

1. recognize money and possessions as means to an end rather than ends in themselves;

2. express appreciation to God for the spiritual blessings received through Christ Jesus their Savior and Lord;

3. seek God's direction and guidance in dealing with financial challenges and dilemmas;

4. demonstrate a desire to honor God with the management of their financial blessings.

▲ Opening Prayer

Invite participants to join you in praying the prayer printed in the Study Guide or lead the group in an extemporaneous prayer, thanking God for His goodness in Christ Jesus and asking the Holy Spirit's blessing upon your study of this lesson.

▲ Focusing Our Attention

As a group, identify all the benefits from God listed in Psalm 103:1–5 for which David offers Him praise. David says, God *forgives all your sins and heals all your diseases, ... redeems your life from the pit ... crowns you with love and*

compassion ... satisfies your desires with good things so that your youth is renewed like the eagle's. Invite participants to share with a partner or in small groups about the item from the list for which they are most thankful today.

▲ Getting Our Perspective

Read the introductory information in this section aloud to the group. Ask, **Why do we often fail to recognize spiritual blessings to be of greater value than material possessions?** Affirm participant responses. Possible responses may include the following: Material things are easy to recognize by sight, they satisfy basic desires and provide a means of measuring progress. Invite participants to work through the numbered items with partners or in small groups. After several minutes reassemble everyone, inviting participants to share insights and comments on each item.

1. a. As the Holy Spirit works in our hearts through the Gospel, He plants in us the desire to live for God and to please Him in every way—including our management of financial resources—as we grow in the knowledge of Him.

b. This verse mentions avoiding interference in the affairs of others and working faithfully to win the respect of those outside the faith and not to be dependent on anyone as evidence of the power of the Gospel at work in believers' lives. Comment that mismanagement of financial affairs and unfaithfulness to occupation or vocation often cause people to become dependent upon others and to lose their respect.

2. Material things are important to all of us. Some material things are necessities for life and effective Christian witness. Of themselves, material things are not bad or harmful. Only when material things are misused or improperly regarded do they threaten or endanger a Christian's witness and growth in the faith.

3. Answers may vary somewhat. Affirm the first and fourth choices as clear examples of the proper application of this biblical principle.

4. Answers may vary. Ask participants to explain their rankings.

5. Responsible Christian stewards, concerned about using their resources to the glory of God, always do well to ask themselves what they are receiving for money that leaves

their hands. Many, placing their hopes on making a big win, have become addicted to gambling.

▲ Money Matters

Ask a volunteer to read the introductory material aloud to the group. Invite participants to share examples of experiences from their own lives or the lives of others that parallel that of Bill and Joannie. Allow participants to work in groups to read and discuss each of the vignettes in this section. Or if time is limited, divide participants into four groups and assign each group a vignette to read and discuss. After allowing time for group work, reassemble for a brief review of each vignette.

Meet Sandy

1. Sandy's situation not only proved her mother to be right, it also placed Sandy in a position where she needed to depend on her mother in order to repair her car.

2. Realizing that what could happen sometimes does, Sandy might take care to avoid impulsive spending and to have money in reserve for emergencies. Comment that being financially strapped limits a person's options for serving God and others.

Meet Cindy and Dan.

1. Affirm participant responses. Most will agree that differences in financial management styles and approaches and differences of opinion over who should be primarily responsible for paying bills, together with conflict over individual expenditures, can result in marital tension and stress.

2. Responses will vary. Cindy and Daniel should be assured that God can bring good out of this stressful situation. As one possible plan of action, Cindy and Daniel might each list their goals and frustrations and then discuss their lists and prayerfully seek a plan of action that will ease their frustrations while moving them closer to their goals.

Meet Mike

1. Credit cards make it easy for people to spend money they don't have, with the idea that they can pay the debt in small monthly installments. Mike discovered how quickly one can get head over heels into debt by using credit cards to increase his purchasing power. By law and conscience, when we owe someone something, we are leashed to them by obligation until we repay them.

2. Using credit cards carries several advantages. Using credit cards eliminates the need to carry large amounts of cash, it consolidates bills into one monthly statement, and many credit cards are accepted worldwide. Only when they are misused do credit cards pose a danger to the carrier's financial well-being.

▲ To Do at Home

Encourage participants to do one or more of these activities during the week ahead.

▲ Closing Prayer

Conclude the session following the suggestion provided in the Study Guide.

Session 5

Living Stewardship

▲ Focus

Show the class a service manual from one of your appliances. Point out that it was written by the one who designed and built the appliance. Say, **When questions arise about the appliance, the manual is the best place to go for answers. Somewhat similarly, the Bible is the best place for Christians to go for God's wisdom and counsel in managing finances and all other aspects of their lives.**

Welcome everyone to the final session of this course. Make sure each participant has a copy of the Study Guide. Briefly review the topics covered in the preceding four sessions. Comment that today's session will wrap things up with a practical look at the family budget.

▲ Objectives

That by the power of the Holy Spirit working through God's Word, the participants will

1. affirm that Jesus our Savior and friend will remain with His followers to guide, strengthen, and sustain them throughout the ups and downs of their lives;

2. demonstrate a desire to honor God as they plan and reach their financial goals;

3. explore one family budgeting plan;

4. recognize the spiritual benefits of seeking God's help, guidance, and direction in managing family finances.

▲ Opening Prayer

Invite participants to join you in praying the prayer printed in the Study Guide, or lead the group in an extemporaneous prayer thanking God for His goodness in Christ Jesus and asking the Holy Spirit's blessing upon your study of this lesson.

▲ Focusing Our Attention

Invite participants to share with partners or in small groups about the grocery items that best describe their approach toward budgeting and financial management.

▲ God Is with Us

Ask a volunteer to read the introductory paragraph aloud to the group. Have participants work with partners or in small groups to read the Bible verses about the life of Joseph and discuss the questions that follow. Then, once again, in a large group invite participants to share comments and insights generated by each of the discussion items.

1. Joseph was blessed because the Lord was with Him. Invite participants to underline the words, *the Lord was with him,* each time they appear in the text.

2. By God's grace, Joseph endured and even thrived in the most disadvantaged of circumstances. His life dramatically illustrates how God never leaves and always provides for

His own—sometimes in ways far beyond our ability to anticipate or comprehend.

3. Affirm responses that center around the concept that
while God does not promise our way will always be easy, He
does promise to remain with us and to strengthen us through
all the highs and lows of our lives.

▲ Financial Planning

Read this section to the group, pausing between paragraphs to reinforce, explain, and comment on what you have
read. Then allow participants to work independently to complete Chart A. Suggest that those who did not bring exact figures with them complete the activity also, estimating
amounts for each category. Suggest that they might find it
interesting to compare later their estimates with the actual
figures.

▲ Points to Ponder

This section is solely for individual reflection. After allowing an adequate amount of time for participants to work
through the questions, invite general comments or insights
individuals may wish to share with the group. Move on to the
next section.

▲ Living Out the Plan

Ask volunteers to take turns reading this section to the
group, paragraph by paragraph. Pause between paragraphs
to add comments and reflections. Invite participants to share
the types of money management systems they use and the
benefits of each approach. Direct attention to Charts B and C
as appropriate. Continue with a whole-group discussion of the
questions at the end of the section.

1. Answers will vary.
2. Answers will vary.

▲ Benefiting from the Plan

Read or paraphrase the opening paragraph. Then continue with a whole-group discussion of the items that follow.

Answers for all items will vary. Reinforce the concept that God's love and care build character and deep spiritual commitment as, working through the Word, He carries us through each of these situations. Invite individuals to share other situations similar to those described in which they have seen the hand of God at work, blessing, encouraging, and sustaining His people.

▲ To Do at Home

Encourage participants prayerfully to evaluate or initiate their own family budget system.

▲ Closing Prayer

Thank participants for joining you for this study. Conclude with the closing provided in the Study Guide.

If your car is a total loss and you need the title to give to your carrier, the process of obtaining reimbursement could also be expedited. The more you can do to speed up the process and protect your interests, the better off you will be.

It is also important, but oftentimes overlooked, that you keep a record of any expenses that you incur and pay for in reference to your car. Whatever the expenses, no matter what the amount, submit them to the carrier and let it advise what is or is not covered. Why should you absorb even the smallest amount—money is money. If the expenses are not covered by your carrier, perhaps you could seek reimbursement through the other driver's carrier.

One of the most important objectives of this book is to make you—the policyholder and consumer—more aware of your rights on insurance claims. Also of great importance is to know your policy and know where to get the answers. Adjusters, though expected to be knowledgeable about medical injuries and terminology, law, and anything else that applies to a claim, cannot know everything. But a good adjuster knows where to look and whom to question for information. The same should apply to you and your policy. Whether it pertains to damage to your automobile, expenses because of the damage or injuries sustained, or understanding why you have been offered a specific amount to accept and settle, you must do your homework to understand what is going on. If you can discipline yourself to accomplish this for insurance, it should carry over into everything else you deal with.

Chapter 4

The Statement

You will probably be required to give a statement to either your carrier or the carrier that insures the other party, or both. Statements can be given in four ways:

Verbal Statement

This is the least used, mostly when liability is completely established, either against you or the other party. The accident could be a rear-ender by either party, without injuries, and as a formality, the company needs to verify the information. The verbal procedure could also be used on a no-claim incident; that is, reported for precautionary measures only. Your carrier will decide.

Company Form

This is what the carrier, either yours or the other party's, will send you to fill out. It will give the carrier basic information about the accident and you the opportunity to describe the accident. If the accident is not serious (perhaps a one-vehicle accident with vehicle damage only), the form will be used. Sometimes the form provides the carrier with enough information to alert it that a further, more detailed investigation is needed. It could then follow up with the recorded or written statement. The company form is similar to what you would have to file with your Registry of Motor Vehicles. Each carrier investigates each claim differently, and what type of form it uses is its decision.

Recorded Statement

When the recorded statement is used, the carrier legally has to tell you that it will be recording the interview. The drawback to a recorded statement is that the questions and responses are given spontaneously. You can ask the adjuster to stop the recorder if you do not understand a question or do not feel comfortable with your answer, which the adjuster must do. This is not the most advantageous way to give a statement, as your recollection of the accident facts can be vague or inaccurate if you are not being questioned within a reasonable amount of time after the accident. If you decide to give a statement in this manner, request a copy. In fact, to verify the accuracy of the statement, you should be able to secure a transcribed copy from the carrier and sign and return it. Make a copy for your records and/or request a copy. It can be unethical if a carrier does not give you a copy of your statement. The recorded statement is generally used by the staff adjuster who works inside the office. It can also be employed if a statement is taken by an adjuster from someone living long distance.

Written Statement

The written statement is the one I find most accurate and popular. Here a representative of the carrier visits you at a place of your choosing. It can be your home, place of employment, or anywhere you feel comfortable. If you have legal representation and your attorney allows you to give a statement, it is generally done at the attorney's office in his/her presence.

My experience has found the person's home the most comfortable; again, if no attorney is involved. I found this type of statement to be the most accurate for a number of reasons. First, it allows the adjuster and person being interviewed to meet face-to-face, helping to relax a tense situation. Second, it allows both parties to discuss the events of the accident before the statement is taken. This not only gives the victim a chance to know what will be asked, but can also assist the adjuster in projecting a clear picture of how the accident occurred. Third, the pace of this statement is slower than a recorded one, and more opportunity is given for discussion as you proceed. Fourth, the person is allowed to read the statement and can then make corrections or additions. You are then asked to sign the statement and should receive a copy. If not, demand it.

The statement is a tool used by the insurance company to determine the facts of the accident and any injuries resulting. It is inadmissible in court, but can be referred to for information. If a claim reaches the point in which it goes into litigation, then depositions are taken. These are statements taken by either the attorney representing you personally or the carrier(s). In this case, you are questioned by the attorney at his/her office and the questions and answers are typed and signed so that the deposition can be entered in court. As long as your recollections are accurate and you are organized in your facts, you should have no fears about giving a statement. If there is no attorney involved, do not refuse to give a statement or allow the insurance company to rely on a police report only. By refusing to give a statement, you could jeopardize your position and force the company to make a decision based on minimal evidence. If an attorney is present, follow the attorney's advice.

In giving a statement to an insurance company, follow these guidelines: A statement should include information about yourself, such as

1. Name
2. Address (advise if this is permanent; if not, the new address)
3. Date of birth
4. Social Security number
5. Driver's license number (list type and restrictions; i.e., the need for corrective lenses, etc.)
6. Occupation and place of employment
7. Marital status and any children
8. Information on your vehicle (owner, year, make, model, VIN, color, plate number, mechanical and body condition, and any lienholder).

You now have the basic information documented and are ready to give the facts of the accident. Remember, all the information you provide will help the carriers determine how the accident occurred. Reconstruct the events leading up to the accident. Companies will be concerned as to whether you were on any medication or had consumed alcohol, and if so, how much. If that is not a factor, begin with the place from which you departed. You may have left your home to go shopping or to work. Note whether or not you were in a rush. Give the names of streets you were traveling on to reach your destination. When you arrive at the accident site, comment on your familiarity with the area and road. Describe the weather conditions that day. Was it sunny, rainy, snowy, and was it necessary to have your windshield wipers or lights on? Comment on the road—was it straight, bending toward one direction or another, hilly up or down? Was the area lit well enough for you to see? Was your view obstructed by trees, shrubs, signs?

One suggestion that may assist you before you give the statement to your company is to recreate the accident. In your mind, retrace your steps from the time you left Point A to the time of the accident and try to remember each detail. You may want to revisit the scene or drive through the route leading up to the accident. You may uncover a fact that you had forgotten. Again, keep in mind that the statement that you give to the police, if it is done at the scene, is done so under some confusion and it is generally condensed. It is recommended that you go to the police station and give a more formal statement, as the initial statement given may not contain all of the details.

Generally, a statement will say, "I was traveling down Elm Street when this other car pulled out from nowhere and struck me." If the insurance company were to use that statement for your testimony, it would not be accurate and leaves open the possibility of many questions. The statement given to the insurance company should be more detailed and accurate, without sounding unintentionally fabricated. By that, I mean that the statement should always be truthful to the best of your knowledge, and the facts you present should support your statement. The adjuster can sometimes determine if your statement coincides with the vehicle damage, witness statements, and initial statement made at the scene.

Comment on the surface and measurement of the road if it is pertinent. This will be useful when you are making your diagram. If you do not have a tape measure, count off the footage by stepping it off. (The average individual covers three feet in one step.) If you are going to recreate the scene or measure distances, do it without jeopardizing yourself. A good time is an early weekend morning, preferably Sunday, when traffic is at its lightest. If you are equipped with a good camera, take photographs of the area. Better yet, try to show how the area appeared at the time of the accident; that is, if it was dusk, dawn, rainy, etc. Your company will probably have photographs taken by one of its adjusters or by an independent, but you can assure this by doing it yourself if it is appropriate and convenient. Show any traffic lights, flashing lights, stop signs, or possibly missing stop or yield signs for you or the other party. The town or city highway or transportation department should have a record if a sign once existed in a particular area and was just never re-erected.

Once you have recreated the events leading up to the accident, you can now state how it happened. Did you look away, drop something, light a cigarette? State if you saw the other party before the accident and what he/she was doing. Keep in mind that you may not be an expert in judging speed, so you cannot expect the allegation that the other party must have been speeding as a cause. If you were aware of the other vehicle's excessive speed, why then did you not let it pass? Likewise, to say that you never saw the other car is assuming that it dropped out of the sky. Show where it came from or it will be interpreted that you did not pay attention. Could you or the other operator have avoided the accident? Try to be as honest as you can. Remember, if the police are able to determine the true facts through their investigation and with the assistance of a witness, these facts could contradict your statement and it will be difficult to prove your case. If you feel that what you stated was accurate, then stick with it. But be honest. Many accident claims could be processed much more quickly if people would admit to their fault and accept the consequences.

Once you have detailed your account of the accident, you can then describe the damage to the vehicles. Basically, the company is interested in the point of impact area—that is, left front on one car and front on the other car—wherever the initial impact occurred. You can then incorporate the entire area of damage to both cars if you took notice, so the company can adjust the cost or "reserves" needed to make repairs, if applicable.

If there were any complaints or signs of injuries, note them. If you were injured, note the diagnosis and who treated you, giving the correct names, addresses, and telephone numbers of the treating facilities. Obviously, if you have this information for other injured individuals, supply this to the carrier as well.

If you paid for towing, car rental, medical treatment, prescriptions, or anything else related to the accident and considered out-of-pocket expenses, note it. You can submit these expenses and let the insurance company advise what is or is not covered.

At this point, you should have a better understanding as to what the carrier will look for when it investigates an accident. Be prepared to give a statement to the police, whether it is at the scene, at the police station, or if they visit you—notably in the hospital. You will also have to file a report with the Registry of Motor Vehicles, depending on the circumstances, cost of damages, and injuries; the police can advise you on this. In any event, the statements you give to them will not be as detailed as the one you give to the carrier, but they should be factual and accurate. Too often people feel that the statement given to the police is sufficient, and they are surprised to see how much detail is contained in the statement taken by the adjuster.

The items contained in a statement which I mentioned and feel are important are a result of my experience in dealing with claims. You may discover other facts that you feel are important, and if so, incorporate them into your statement. The goal of any insurance company, adjuster, or agent should be to obtain as many facts as possible. They should welcome the policyholders' involvement so that all parties can benefit by working together.

Diagram

To emphasize your point of view about the facts of the accident, prepare a diagram to correlate with your statement. In order to make your diagram as accurate as possible, you can go to any art supply store and purchase a template, which costs only a few dollars. If you have to file a report with the Registry, send a copy of your diagram as well as your statement.

The adjuster may also prepare a diagram during your meeting and have you sign it.

For your benefit, I have included a sample written statement and diagram of the accident scene.

Sample Written Statement—
Automobile Claim

The following is a sample statement in reference to an automobile accident.

STATEMENT

I am Joseph G. Sarro. I reside at 110 Blue Moon Terrace, Anytown, Rhode Island 02000. Telephone (111) 222-3333. This is a permanent address and telephone number, and I have resided here for 8 years. I am 36 years of age (d.o.b. 11/2/53). SS# 012-12-1212. Driver's license number for the state of Rhode Island is 5555555 with no restrictions. I am 5'8" tall and weigh 145 lbs. I am single with no dependents. I am self-employed as a business owner, the company being "The Family Tree." This is a florist shop located at 23 Jones Street, Anytown, R.I. 02999. Telephone (112) 223-3334. I have owned this business for two (2) years and its hours are Monday through Friday, 9:00 A.M. to 5:00 P.M. It is closed Saturdays and Sundays.

I own only one vehicle, a personal vehicle, identified as a 1985 Ford Escort, color blue, R.I. Plate FMTREE. There was no previous damage to this vehicle before June 6, 1988. The vehicle was well-maintained and serviced by John's Service Station, Anytown, R.I.

On June 6, 1988, the date of the accident, I was driving to work in my vehicle with no passengers. The time of the accident was approximately 8:10 A.M. I am fairly sure of the time because I had my radio on and the time was mentioned. The weather was sunny, clear, good visibility, and the roads were dry. The sun did not obstruct my view, and I was traveling on an asphalt-surfaced road.

I had left my home and traveled north to Route 26, also known as William Street, Anytown, R.I. The accident occurred on William Street, which is a four (4)-lane road, two lanes in each direction, going north to south. I was traveling south in the inner lane, the lane closest to the sidewalk. The north and southbound lanes are separated by a grassy median, the southbound lanes by dotted lines. Traffic was moderate at the time for my direction of travel. By moderate, I mean that there were cars in front and behind me in both lanes but a good distance apart, about two car lengths at least. There was no obstruction on the road, nor any construction, and no police were in the area. I was proceeding at a speed of approximately 45 mph, and the speed limit is 40 mph. The cars in front of me and beside me were maintaining the same distance, so I would estimate their speed to be about the same.

I had been on Route 26 for about 5 miles with the circumstances remaining the same. Suddenly, the car to my left, which was nearly even with me, sped up and entered my lane without warning. I can only believe that the operator had seen his exit approaching in the next one-half mile and did not want to miss it. This is what was stated after the accident when I spoke with the other operator. The car in question, a 1987 Buick Regal, color brown, R.I. Plate 115330, pulled into my lane so quickly that there was no time to react. The Buick struck my vehicle with its right front fender in the left front. The impact pushed my vehicle against the curb, where I was able to maintain control. After impact, the Buick continued into my lane, and I followed it as we both took the upcoming exit ramp, then pulled into a parking lot.

The operator of the car that struck mine was James James, 135 James Street, Anytown, R.I. He was alone at the time. Neither myself nor Mr. James complained of or showed signs of being injured. I called the local police for that town and one officer arrived within 15 minutes. He took down the information that Mr. James and I exchanged and then left. Both vehicles were drivable after the accident and driven away by the same operators. I continued on my way to work, as did Mr. James, who works at Thomases Lumberyard, Newtown, R.I. Mr. James also stated that he had coverage on his vehicle.

As far as I know, there were no witnesses to the accident who stopped and gave their names to either operator or the police. Also, neither operator received a citation. No alcohol or drugs were involved.

My vehicle has already been seen at Tom's Auto Body and damages amount to $750.00.

I am not represented by an attorney for this accident. I have been driving since the age of 17 and this is my first accident.

I have read the above two pages, they are true to the best of my knowledge, and I have received a copy.

SIGNATURE:_____ DATE:____

Since liability in this case appears to be on Mr. James solely, his carrier would be in a position to pay for your damages, and this would be filed for reporting purposes only, unless you wished to be paid by your carrier under collision coverage.

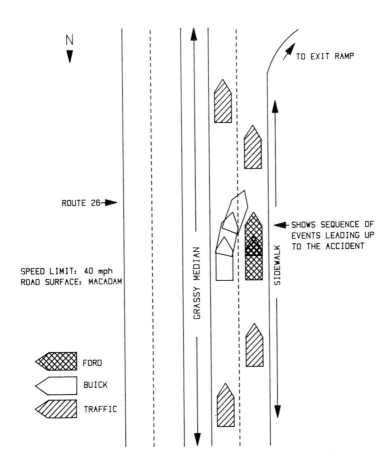

N

TO EXIT RAMP

ROUTE 26

SHOWS SEQUENCE OF
EVENTS LEADING UP
TO THE ACCIDENT

GRASSY MEDIAN

SIDEWALK

SPEED LIMIT: 40 mph
ROAD SURFACE: MACADAM

FORD

BUICK

TRAFFIC

Diagram is according to statement of operator. It should be drawn and
signed by the operator signifying accuracy.

Chapter 5

Injury Claim

This chapter will discuss the evaluation of a minor injury claim that would not involve the services of an attorney—a claim which you would feel comfortable in attempting to settle yourself.

If you are injured as a result of an automobile accident, you can submit a claim whether you are the operator, passenger, or pedestrian. If you are the operator or passenger in Vehicle 1, the claim would be directed toward the coverage on that vehicle. If the other vehicle, Vehicle 2, has coverage, your claim could go toward that coverage. What determines who covers the claims? Since laws are different for every state, your concern should be to notify the carrier(s) involved of your injury and its extent. They then have to determine liability from the police reports, statements, etc., and they can determine which operator was at fault. That does not help you in the meantime, so it is important that they be aware of your injury and you proceed toward recuperation. Once the responsible carrier is determined, it can follow up for your medical discharge and attempt to settle your claim.

If you are a passenger in any vehicle, you are 100 percent free of negligence *unless it can be proven that as a passenger you contributed to the accident; i.e., pulling at the steering wheel or blinding the operator.* Otherwise, you have no problem with liability. Your claim would then be directed against the liable operator, either the operator of the car in which you were a passenger or the other operator.

In any case, the carrier should explain what your rights are as an injured party and the laws of the state in which the accident occurred.

Medical Expenses

First, you establish the total amount of your medical expenses, including any unpaid bills and bills paid by a health carrier or by yourself. However, any expenses which have already been paid by the automobile carrier should be excluded to avoid double payment. The automobile coverage is considered the primary coverage in an automobile accident. Any other coverage, such as Blue Cross or Medicare, could and would seek reimbursement by filing a lien if it paid the bills initially. If the health carrier does not file a lien, it could contact you at some point after the claim is settled, looking for reimbursement. You could be responsible for the bill in question if the amount was not included in the settlement and you signed a release with the insurance carrier. This will be discussed further in another chapter. Also note that if you were working at the time of the incident, Workers' Compensation could be the primary carrier.

In summation, in this first category you include the following under medical expenses: treatment, prescriptions, crutches, neckbraces, special shoes, or whatever is prescribed by your doctor to make you well.

Loss of Earnings

In the second category, you would include lost income or loss of earning capacity. In claiming loss of earnings, you are submitting your gross earnings lost as a result of the accident. Normally, the carrier will secure this information from your employer, accountant, or previous tax records. All information should be available to the carrier if it is to be claimed. It should also be noted that whether you work one, two, or three jobs, lost earnings from them are included in the total amount to be reimbursed. If you were preparing to start a job or can prove that you were seeking employment but the accident prevented you from doing so, and someone had an interest in hiring you, then this would fall under the loss of earning capacity. The wage loss information is then added to your medical expenses.

Disability

The third category is for disability, more commonly referred to as "pain and suffering." If you can show injury or prove disability even though no medical treatment was involved, then you would be entitled to pain and suffering compensation in addition to the above-mentioned categories. If no treatment were involved, it could be that you continued to work in discomfort and felt that the pain would subside after a few days, or you dislike medical treatment and chose not to see a doctor. Just because you do not receive medical treatment, this does not preclude you from seeking reimbursement if you can prove the pain existed. Obviously, it is easier to prove if there is treatment.

There are generally three types of disability designated by the insurance companies: (1) Total Disability, (2) Partial Disability, and (3) Pain and Suffering.

Total Disability

Total Disability is that period of time when you were incapable of performing your normal activities as a result of your injury. As an example, if you work a forty-hour week and were unable to work at all, you would be considered totally disabled. Your doctor will instruct you on what you can and cannot do and will include this information in his/her report to the carrier. The report should also indicate whether or not you are totally disabled.

Partial Disability

When partially disabled, you are able to perform your activities but are limited. For example, if instead of the usual forty hours per week you work approximately 15–20 hours, you would be in this category. There may be occasions when the doctor will allow you to return to your job but may reduce the time for one reason or another, and thus your work capacity is reduced. You may not be able to perform your housework at 100 percent capacity, so you may have to limit your housework time or hire someone to come in and temporarily help. The expense of having to hire someone to do this is covered.

In this instance, you are able to work your normal period but are doing so in pain. Possibly it is because the injury is not severe enough to prevent you from working but you experience pain frequently and/or occasionally.

The above information is to be used as a guideline in evaluating claims. I recall an insurance educational class in which the proctor asked members of the class their opinions as to how they would evaluate a particular claim. The class was made up of adjusters from all parts of the United States and Canada. They were asked to put a dollar figure on an injury claim. For ten people the proctor questioned, he received at least eight different responses. In other words, carriers apply their own method of evaluation, but it generally falls into the categories mentioned above. There is also a difference in the amount of money carriers apply toward total and partial disability and pain and suffering. That depends on the type of injury—whether it be a soft tissue, such as a muscle sprain, or worse, such as a fracture. Today, carriers are evaluating injuries based on their seriousness, which increases the worth of the disability.

Evaluating Your Claim

To give you an example of how one company may evaluate a claim, I submit the following:

Say your medical expenses are $1,000 and your lost

wages for five weeks total $1,500. That totals $2,500 for these two categories.

Next is the evaluating of your disability. If the company were to classify you as totally disabled, it may allow you $300 a week for the five weeks that you were out of work. Adding this figure ($1,500) to the $2,500, your claim would be worth $4,000. This example is based on a minor injury, meaning that the individual was able to return to work without any future problems. Also, the figure of $300 is used in this example, but it could be higher or lower in other instances. If an attorney were involved in representing you, the figure could be raised to $400 or $500, but that includes the attorney's fee, which is one-third of the amount of the entire claim.

If the person's injury were a fracture to a hand, foot, or finger and you use the same amounts for the medicals and wages, and if the disability period is established by the doctor, the figure for disability could be higher. This is taking into consideration that there is no attorney involved. The seriousness of the injury could allow the carrier to raise the figure of disability. The determination depends on the carrier, its geographical location (the claim office), and, obviously, the figures it uses.

When you are in a situation in which you are going to handle your own claim without legal representation, have the adjuster explain the amount being offered. The only guideline the company uses is based on past court rulings and a general consensus of what other carriers use. You will not find the adjuster showing you a book that states this is what is used to evaluate and it must be obeyed.

The above information is this writer's opinion, based on experience. It also pertains to minor injuries and disability in which you feel comfortable in handling your own claim. If your injuries are such that they require lengthy or permanent treatment, you may wish to consult an attorney. If you would like to attempt settlement on your own, apply my formula using the sum totals of medical expenses, lost wages or earnings, and the number of days and/or weeks you were disabled. The state in which I was an adjuster indicated that the insurance companies generally use $300–$400 for total, $100–$200 for partial, and $50–$150 for pain and suffering.

If the injury were to require hospitalization, the total disability could increase to $500–$600 a week, or even more. If you suffered a permanent injury and/or scarring, then this would be additional compensation above and beyond.

Legal Representation

Don't be afraid to deal with an insurance company on an injury. Have it explain how it arrives at any figure offered for settlement. If your figures and those of the adjusters are different, but close, then you should be able to resolve the matter amicably. If the figures are too distant, see where the discrepancies are and why. If there is permanent injury and/or scarring, you may want to engage the services of an attorney. The determination of these special injuries are too varied to pinpoint and evaluate so I can only suggest you check previous court rulings on settlements of the same type of injury to see what was awarded. (This is if you want to handle your own claim.)

Because attorneys are involved in these matters daily, they are more able to settle the claim for its true worth. You could always have the adjuster submit the figure and its breakdown and reach agreement by that means. However, you would have no previous data on which to determine whether or not the figure is fair and accurate. You could also show the figures to an attorney for an opinion if he/she is a friend. If the claim is small enough and the figures accurate, chances are the attorney may not bother to get legally involved.

Chapter 6

Releases

In any type of accident, the release is the ultimate goal. Releases come under several different categories and may be entitled "General Release," "Husband and Wife Release," "Parent/Guardian Release," or "Uninsured Motorist Release."

Carriers ask that you read the release before you sign it, and well you should. Question what the wording means, and you may find sometimes that the adjuster is unsure. It is written in a legal form that is often read too quickly or not at all.

Basically, a release states that the person signing it is doing so knowing that he/she is settling the claim for financial consideration. The figure has already been agreed upon and once the release is signed, and sometimes notarized, the person will receive the money. There are times when the release should be notarized, and on this question, you can consult an attorney or notary public. Normally, the release is just signed and witnessed. The witness can be the adjuster, a family member, a friend, or anyone of your choosing.

Once you have signed the release, it is the company's understanding that your claim is settled. You cannot make further claim against the company and person you are releasing as long as their identities are on the release. You should be aware that the money you are receiving covers settlement of the claim and all the expenses, paid and unpaid, *present and future.* That is why, as stated earlier, you should make sure that all bills and expenses are included in your claim and the settlement. You want to avoid a medical bill you thought was paid but later surfaces. Likewise, if Blue Cross has paid a bill, make sure that amount is included in the settlement, as the company could come to you for payment. If you should contact the insurance carrier months later to pay a medical bill, it may tell you that the case is settled and the bill is your responsibility.

You could also have two claims with the company—one for your vehicle (property damage) and one for your injury (bodily injury). One release you sign may apply to your vehicle damage only, in which case your injury claim is still open. You must fully understand exactly what you are signing and why. Make sure the release for the property damage specifies that it is for property damage and the release for the bodily injury specifies that it is for bodily injury. Ask questions about the release and make a copy for your records.

On those cases that you feel that you can handle, dealing with the adjuster can be both educational and rewarding. On those cases in which you prefer the representation of legal counsel, a lawyer will handle the responsibility and can explain the release if it becomes too complicated. Settle your claim for what you feel is a fair and accurately explained figure. Remember that a release, in the carrier's opinion, is final. If you feel that you have been misinformed by the adjuster or carrier after you have signed the release, the release can be questioned as to whether it was obtained in good faith. If you ever reach that point in your claim, consult an attorney immediately. Too often, people are advised that they will receive money if they just sign the release. A quick dollar can sometimes cloud the situation, and thus settlement of a claim is made prematurely.

Before you sign the release, make sure that the legally required number of days have passed before it is signed or executed. Some states require that thirty days from the date of the accident pass before signing in reference to an injury claim. The release could be considered invalid if signed in less time than that. This amount of time is given for a number of reasons. It is established to protect the injured, as it allows for discovery and/or diagnosis of any injury, and it prevents the carrier from escaping medical expenses by settling a claim too quickly. You don't want to be in a position in which you have signed the release and the injury activates or reactivates, requiring further treatment and/or lost time from work. You would then have to absorb the additional expenses yourself. Only a physician or qualified medical expert can state if you are discharged or not, and you should not sign a release until then.

One other item of interest: If you are involved in an automobile accident in which the injuries are very serious in nature and it leads to settlement, your claim may settle for the policy limits of the other vehicle, but the limit may be less than the value of your claim. When the carrier evaluates your claim, even if it feels that the claim is worth more than the limits on the policy, it will only pay the policy limit. The name of the carrier and the owner/operator of the other vehicle will be on the release in this instance.

You will want to check the assets of the owner/operator to see if he/she is financially able to pay the remainder of what your claim is worth. You will probably make a claim under your policy, but to protect the interest of yourself and your company, the name of the carrier only should be on the release. If the owner is financially solid to pay you without any delay, then an action can be started against the owner/operator. If the claim should be serious enough to reach this point, it is advisable to obtain the services of an attorney. Normally, the excess amount will be sought from your carrier as it has the money on hand.

You must advise your carrier of the fact that the other carrier is offering you its policy limits. Your carrier will have to permit the settlement if you are going to pursue the claim against it. It just protects the company's position in handling the claim if it pursues subrogation (reimbursement) from the other owner/operator. Otherwise, if you are satisfied with the amount of money and it is equivalent to your damages, be they property damage or bodily injury, and if you have read and understood the release, then signing the release should pose no problem.

Chapter 7

Accident with Death Resulting

If you or a member of your family is involved in an automobile accident and dies as a result, it will have to be decided whether or not to retain legal counsel. Every state has enacted what is referred to as the "Wrongful Death" statute. It means that the surviving spouse, children, or parents may recover money (also known as damages) from the party found to be responsible or negligent for that person's death. Be aware of the statute in your state, as they do differ from state to state.

Negligence may be found to be that of the operator of the other vehicle or the operator of the vehicle in which your family member was a passenger (whether it be your vehicle or someone else's). The amount that you can recover varies in each state and the figure is not difficult to verify; contact your insurance commissioner to ascertain it. Other factors determine the value of the claim, such as the person's life expectancy and earning capacity.

It also has to be determined if the deceased suffered from conscious pain and suffering. This would pertain to the length of time the person lived until he/she was pronounced dead and if consciousness was achieved to the point in which the person was aware of his/her condition.

The insurance company will secure the death certifi-

:ate and you will want to be aware of the medical examiner's findings to determine the exact cause of death. Traces of drugs and/or alcohol could be found, or the death may have stemmed from a heart attack. This information must be determined to allow the insurance company to fairly evaluate the claim for damages.

I realize that this is not the easiest task to perform when you are faced with the death of a loved one. However, with automobile accidents contributing so greatly to deaths on our highways, we all must be prepared to deal with the possibility of this unfortunate tragedy. If the situation becomes too emotionally distressing and complex to handle, then it is advisable to seek legal counsel.

The insurance company will conduct its investigation and evaluate the claim depending on its findings. The major factor in this type of claim is the police investigation and witness statements. However, under the Wrongful Death statute, the insurance company may even ultimately settle for an amount which is generally the minimum amount it can owe, even if found not to be totally at fault. If you are faced with a situation in which the other vehicle is at fault and the carrier for that vehicle agrees to settle the claim, it does not prevent you from pursuing a claim against the company that insures your vehicle. You would have to determine that the value of the claim is more than what was settled for by the other carrier, which in these cases would amount to its policy limits. You would then pursue a claim against the company of the deceased, and this would be designated as an "underinsured claim."

Chapter 8

Helpful Hints when Dealing with an Automobile Claim

When you are involved in an automobile accident, here are some hints to help prepare and protect yourself.

Property Damage

One way to prepare for the prospect of your car being damaged is to have a reputable auto body shop on your list of contacts. Select a shop with a good reputation for quality, timely results. You may be able to find a shop that also operates a towing business. If you have rental coverage, check with your auto body repairer to see if it rents vehicles. The more contacts you have available in case of a mishap, the less running around you have to do and the less stress you will encounter, especially if your time is limited.

Once the vehicle has been taken to the repair shop, the insurance adjuster will appraise the damage in person and reach an agreed price with the shop. Repairs can begin as soon as clearance has been given by the carrier. Although you may authorize the repairs to begin prior to the adjuster's appraisal of the vehicle, the damage could be questioned by the adjuster if it has been repaired before he/she views it.

If your car is appraised as a total loss, here are a few steps you can take to ensure a fair settlement:

Determine the Value of the Vehicle

Check the NADA (National Automobile Dealer's Association) and Red Book, which lists the value of the vehicle, as long as the vehicle is fairly new and still listed. The carrier will use these or similar references to arrive at an "actual cash value" for your car. The book will add and deduct for certain items such as air-conditioning, automatic/manual transmission, sunroof, low/high mileage, etc. These books are available at a car dealer, auto body shop, your carrier, your agent, the bank that may have financed your car, or even the town/city hall.

Obtaining the information from one or both of the aforementioned books gives you one or two value estimates. To obtain further figures, check the newspapers for a car identical to yours and also check two or three dealers. You should have at least four or five figures.

You would then add these figures and divide by the number of sources to obtain the average value of your car. Not only will you have a better idea of the value of your car, but in checking with the dealers, you might be able to find a similar car to purchase, as you will undoubtedly need one.

If you can obtain several figures on the car's value, you should be in the general area of the carrier's appraiser. If there should be a discrepancy, meet with your company's representative or ask for a copy of its appraisal, which you should receive anyway, to determine the difference.

Disposal of the Vehicle

When you finally settle with the carrier on the loss, it will take possession of the vehicle and dispose of it, so it will need all the keys and the title, correctly endorsed. Since the carrier knows the car is a total loss, it does not want to run the risk of having you drive it in the damaged condition and risk another accident. Your carrier will tow the car from the body shop, service station, or wherever it was taken after the accident and it will be taken to an auto placement yard. This yard stores these cars, which are then sold for salvage and the money paid to the insurance company, which also pays the storage company.

If it is the other carrier that settles with you, as a general rule it will not take the car. It will instead deduct the salvage value off the actual cash value of your car, and you will have to dispose of the vehicle. This can work out to your advantage, as the salvage value is sometimes not that high and the car could be sold as is or for parts when the return could be higher than what the company deducted off the final value. Run an ad or contact a salvage yard to take the car. Sometimes an auto bodyshop or service station can use the car for parts. If you owe money for storage or rental and are not being reimbursed for these, you could work out an arrangement in which the car is swapped for the expenses.

Tax Credit

Also be aware of a tax credit available to you if your car is totaled. When you settle with the carrier, they will give you a tax credit letter stating what the settlement of the car was. If you bring this letter with you when you register your next car, the Registry of Motor Vehicles will apply this toward the registration fee. In some states, the tax is added to the settlement figure.

Stolen Vehicle

Note that if your vehicle is stolen and never recovered or is damaged beyond repair because of the theft, the total loss would apply in evaluating your car toward settlement. Also, on a theft in which the car is not recovered, the insurance company has the right to wait thirty days to settle, as it wants to verify that the car is not recovered.

If there is a lienholder on the vehicle, the payment will be made out to you and the lienholder, as the lienholder has the title and an insurable interest in your car.

It is also a good idea to photocopy your registration, bill of sale, and title, as sometimes this information is kept in the glove compartment and if the car is stolen and never recovered or burned, you will have to request copies of these documents, and that could take time. You might want to keep an updated photograph of your car with these other documents, as well as service records, and have these notarized for unquestioning proof for the carrier.

Remember, claim any personal items inside your vehicle which were stolen or damaged at the time of the mishap, and let the carrier advise what is and is not covered. Those not covered could be submitted under your homeowner's policy.

Chapter 9

Precautions

Over the course of my twenty-two years of driving and fourteen years as an insurance adjuster, my experiences have educated me as far as taking necessary precautions to avoid an accident. The precautions listed below should be taken in order to avoid an automobile accident and minimize its devastating impact if one should occur.

1. *Never exceed the posted speed limit.* These limits have been posted for a reason and after careful research. (It is also essential in verifying what your speed was prior to or at the time of the accident.)
2. *Never tailgate.* This applies to all roads—back roads, side streets, and major highways. Here is a good rule to follow in order to determine if you have enough braking distance if the vehicle in front of you should suddenly stop: Pick a point or object that the vehicle in front has just passed. It should take you three seconds to reach that same point (counting one thousand one, one thousand two, one thousand three). If you arrive at that point sooner, then you decrease your chances of being able to stop in an emergency. If you are driving in inclement weather (rainy, snowy, icy), increase the amount of time. You can never be over-

cautious, and the end result if you are not careful is possible injury to persons in the other vehicle or in yours.

3. *Never alert a speeding driver that the police are nearby.* You may think that you are saving someone from receiving a ticket, but this could have devastating results. The car could be stolen, the driver could be under the legal age to drive, or the driver could be intoxicated or on drugs or medication. Allowing the speeder to escape is just as harmful. Think about it! Suppose that person is warned by you and escapes receiving a ticket. Human nature indicates that the operator will not learn from this instance that it was wrong to speed, only that the system was beaten. That same person becomes a very high risk of being involved in an accident because of speeding. It could then cost the operator or people in other vehicles their lives. On the other hand, if the person were to receive a ticket, the possibility for loss of license, increased insurance rates, or, most importantly, what could lead to fatal results might have that person thinking and it could save a life.

4. *Traffic Lights:* If you are at a red traffic light and it turns green, allow yourself two or three seconds before entering the intersection. This allows any vehicles to pass through in case the operator fails to recognize the red light or an emergency vehicle is trying to pass through the intersection. Don't assume that the other operators see the traffic light or stop/yield signs. The sign could be partially hidden, the sun could be a factor, or the person just may not be paying attention.

5. *Seat Belts:* The use of seat belts could save you from substantial injury or even death. If you would like some information on the pros and cons of wearing

seat belts, check with your Registry of Motor Vehicles for studies. If it's the law to wear one in your state, then you must wear a seat belt, but if it is not, use your judgment.

6. *Vehicle Maintenance:* Make sure your vehicle is in good mechanical and electrical operation—periodically check the tires, lights, brakes, horn, windshield wipers, flashers, etc. It's a good idea to take a course in preventive maintenance, or purchase a repair manual for your car. It's also a great idea to have a safety kit in the car at all times, including flashlights, flares, warning devices, first aid kit, water, oil, electrical tape (for repair of hoses), basic tools, and a workable tire jack.

7. *Insurance Agent/Carrier Identification:* Make it a point to know the name of your agent as well as the insurance carrier, and have this information available in the car. When I asked people with claims who they were insured by, most could recall the agent's identity but not the name of their carrier. If you know the name of the carrier, you can immediately report an accident to the carrier without going through the agent, and the investigative process can be expedited. Give the insurance carrier the facts of the accident as well as the identity of the injured and injuries sustained. Also, it is not necessary to withhold information regarding the identity of your insurance company. Whether you are at fault in the accident or not, the other party will eventually determine who the carrier is.

8. *Driving under the Influence:* Remember that as the operator of a vehicle, you have the responsibility of ensuring the safety of your passengers as well as other individuals on the road. Drive cautiously and defensively, and never drive under the influence of alcohol,

drugs, or medication. Be courteous and avoid any altercation with other operators on the road.

9. *Turn Signals:* When preparing to make a turn with your vehicle, always use your turn signal to alert any oncoming traffic or traffic in back of you, and activate it at least one block from your turn. Putting your signal on less than this distance could result in being rear-ended. Make sure your blinker is turned off after making your turn to avoid any confusion as to whether or not you will be turning again. If your turn signal does not function, use hand signals until you have had a chance to fix it. Just to refresh your memory, extending your arm straight out signals a left turn, and the arm bent at the elbow with the hand toward the sky indicates a right turn.

10. *Tailgating:* You are traveling on a country road taking your time and not in any rush. A car that was in the distance suddenly is right behind you and tailgating. Do you increase your speed, quickly apply your brakes, or just become aggravated? The best thing to do is put your right turn signal on and slowly pull over, allowing the other car to pass. By pulling over, you allow the person behind to pass you and continue on his/her way and you to continue safely along. If there are a number of cars behind, then you have the choice of allowing them all to pass or increasing your speed, but within the speed limit posted. The point that I am trying to make is not to become aggravated, causing you to speed up and risk an accident. Let them pass and you will feel more comfortable and less likely to cause an accident, especially if you are unfamiliar with the area.

11. *Courtesy:* Be polite at intersections controlled by four-way stop signs and be cautious at intersections without

any traffic controls. Never assume that the other operator knows what you intend to do. You both may assume the other is stopping, neither does, and you both collide. My rule of driving in these types of situations is to allow the other operators the right-of-way. Drive defensively, and you decrease your chances of an accident. This is a good rule to follow, especially if you are in a densely populated area and there are playgrounds and athletic sites nearby. By allowing the traffic to pass, it also gives you time to view the intersection for bicyclists, motorcyclists, or joggers.

12. *Caution:* When you see someone stopped at the end of a street and you are ready to pass by, it's always possible that the person might just pull out in front of or into you. One way I prepare for this is to note any movement in the front wheel (obviously facing you). If it moves, then you know that person is anxious. Sound your horn, slow down, but get the person's attention. Often someone will be looking for traffic from the other direction while they slowly pull out into your lane or don't even look your way and then slowly pull out. It is sometimes tough to tell when a car is moving just from the observance of the vehicle itself. By seeing the tire move, you will know for sure. Then you can anticipate and act accordingly.

What I am trying to emphasize the most is defensive driving. Be prepared and expect the unexpected. You will drive more intelligently, cautiously, and not take other drivers' mistakes personally.

Chapter 10

Homeowner's Policy

Whether you own a home or condominium or rent an apartment, you should have insurance coverage in case of fire, burglary, or vandalism.

Renting

For the person who rents or leases the property, your coverage would include your personal property and liability. You can insure your personal property and that is a sure way to collect on any damage, even if the building where you reside has coverage also. If your apartment is burglarized, vandalized, or damaged by fire, you would have the coverage to replace your personal possessions. If it were determined by your insurance company that the landlord was negligent in causing the loss, then it would subrogate from the landlord and/or his insurance company after paying you.

Homeowner

For those who own a home or condominium, the insurance coverage includes (1) Dwelling Protection, (2) Personal Property, (3) Family Liability, and (4) Guest Medical Payments. Each insurance company may designate these coverages with these titles or coded with other letters. Your Declarations page will list the coverages along with the amount of your limits of liability.

Coverage on Your Dwelling

The coverage for your dwelling covers the property that you are insuring, example being a home you just purchased. The insurance company will send a representative to appraise your home and determine the value of replacing it if it should be damaged beyond repair. Note that the coverages that you have are listed in your policy. Normally, the company will suggest that you insure your home for 80 percent of its replacement value. For example, say your company has appraised the value at $100,000 (again, this is the replacement value and not the resale value). You would be obligated to carry 80 percent of this amount, or $80,000, to insure replacement cost.

You have to be aware of thé increasing value of your home and make sure that the figure you insure it for is increased properly. Normally, your company will raise the value a percentage each year, but this figure must be in tune with inflation and the cost of building materials. Otherwise if you should suffer a loss that destroys your home, you could receive an amount less than the actual cost of replacing the home at the time of the loss. Today, policies have an "inflation guard," which raises the coverage of your home each year to coincide with inflation. This figure applies to your dwelling and personal property. Your personal property is generally one-half the amount of coverage on your dwelling. For example, if your dwelling is insured for $120,000.00 your personal property would carry $60,000.00 worth of coverage. Ask your agent for the explanation if you are unsure.

Keep in mind that the carrier and agent will ultimately decide on the amount of coverage. It is possible you own a home in a "red-letter" or high-risk area—an area where fires and vandalism are frequent and damaged buildings are located. You may have also purchased the home for say $75,000, but to rebuild it would cost $200,000 because of the construction used in earlier days. Your company will then decide the amount of coverage necessary to protect you. Again, I must point out the importance of communication between you and your agent. Ask questions and offer as much information as you can. There are different policies affording you generally the same type of coverage, but also specifying exclusions which may prevent you from collecting on a claim.

Concerning the adequate amount of insurance for your home structurewise, have the insurance representative, usually the agent, explain how he/she arrived at the figure. Keep in mind that the appraisal is done on the present condition of the home. If your home is in need of repairs or renovations are in the process, the agent may only insure it for its present appearance. Once the improvements have been completed, contact your agent for another appraisal, which should increase the original figure, and the coverage can then be raised.

Personal Property Coverage

In reference to your personal property, as I stated earlier, this figure is normally half the value of the protection you carry on your home. It can be raised with a special endorsement. If you have items of value such as jewelry, furs, or antiques, then these items can be listed for their actual cash value, with an additional premium, on what is called a "floater." Simply stated, any items that are of any real value should be inserted on the floater. Suppose you suffer a burglary and all of your jewelry is stolen; without the special items on this floater, the jewelry will be subject to the limit of coverage on the policy, which can be $1,000 on some policies, regardless of the jewelry's actual value. But say you insured a ring for $2,000 on the floater; you would receive the $2,000 or the same exact ring if the carrier chooses to attempt to replace it.

In order to insure special items, you should take the following into consideration: First, hire a reputable certified appraiser. You can secure the name of one from your agent, telephone book, or the Better Business Bureau and have the items in your home appraised. It should not cost you that much for the initial fee, but whatever it is, it will be worth it. The appraiser can specialize in jewelry, antiques, guns, furs, furniture, clothes, etc. You may have something that has more sentimental value than cash value, and you should use your discretion when insuring these items on a floater.

Once you have gone through this process, you will receive a copy of the appraisal. Have it notarized and present it to your agent, who can make a copy of it and insure the item. As stated earlier, to insure anything under the floater will cost you more in your premium. But why take the risk of losing an item that may have significant value and sentimentality. Compare the difference in the amount of the premium you pay for the policy without the floater and with the floater against the value of the items, and you may feel it's worth it. If you were to lose that item or if it were stolen or destroyed and nonreplaceable, to receive less than the value would be added regret.

Along with the appraisal, it is a good idea to have color photographs of the items, from different angles if necessary. This will not only document more proof of the item's existence, but will also give the insurance company and police a vivid picture of what the item looks like. For the insurance company, it could mean making it easier to have the item replaced if it or you so chooses. Your policy states that the company reimburses you for the amount of the item, if one can be found in the exact likeness, kind, and quality. By having the photograph and appraisal, you also increase your chances of replacing the item. It gives the police a chance of recovery as well as apprehending the thief/thieves. It is in your best interest to keep the appraisal and photographs in a safe place, such as a safety deposit box. In fact, keep a few appraisals and photographs on hand in case they become lost or stolen.

Whether you are going to insure some items on the floater or not, it is a good idea to list the items in your home or apartment and keep this list in a safe location as well. The most accurate way that I have found to obtain a good descriptive list is to break down the items into different categories, room by room, and have it contain the following:

1. Specific description of the item and how many if more than one.
2. Specify where you purchased the item or if it was a gift and from whom and when. If the item was a gift and of worthwhile value, you may want to have a short note from the person stating when the item was given to you, where it was purchased, and the price, as well as a good description.

3. If you purchased the item, give the amount you paid and how paid (cash, check, credit card).
4. Get a price on how much the item cost at the time you submit your claim and the place you secured the price, perhaps from where it was purchased previously. That business may have a copy of your original receipt or it can give you a receipt with the replacement cost.
5. In reference to the above, *keep all receipts* of those items' worth value. This will act as proof positive and keep your claim from dragging. Again, it is up to the individual on the records he/she keeps. Maintain some type of organizational tool to keep your receipts, putting them in their safe place right after you have made the purchase. Not only will you be keeping a record of items for insurance purposes, but also in case there is a problem with the item and it has to be returned, and a record is kept if you want to apply it to your income tax as a deduction.
6. It is very important that you secure a replacement cost on the item. Your policy may allow you to receive "replacement cost" on the item, and the cost in the premium is sometimes extra. If you have this coverage (check with your agent), then you are entitled to replacement cost of that item. If you purchased the item in question five years ago at a cost of $1,000 and it would now cost $2,000 to replace it, you would receive the replacement cost.

Depending on the type of policy you have, depreciation is sometimes applied to the item after securing its replacement cost. Again, I advise you to check with your agent for clarification on this point. Depreciation means that items that do go up in value are subject to being reduced in value. It depends on the item, the age, and the number of years it is determined to last.

Example: Your television was bought three years ago at a cost of $700. At the time of the loss, the same item would sell for $850. Because the television has a life expectancy of approximately ten years, the adjuster will apply 30 percent depreciation to the cost of the replacement. Thus, the value of the television now computes to $850 less 30 percent ($255), reducing the value to $545. If you pay for full replacement coverage, then you may receive $850. If not, then you may receive the $545 less the deductible, which applies in both instances. Keep in mind that as a general rule, insurance companies follow the same basic format in evaluating depreciation. They would have to if they are to keep the principles of settlement understandable for their own staff and policyholders.

How to Handle a Claim

When you are faced with a possible homeowner's claim, consult your policy, define what type of loss you have encountered, and then contact your agent or carrier immediately. As stipulated in your policy and as part of the contract you have with your insurance carrier, you must notify the police as well if the loss is a burglary, attempted break-in, property stolen from your garage while the door is open thereby showing no signs of forced entry, vandalism to your property, or any other mishap which is civil- or criminal-related. Otherwise, the claim will not be processed as complete and it will delay payment to you. The only time you may *not* have to contact the police is if your home had suffered natural damage or if someone should have become injured on your property accidentally.

Determining What Is and Is Not Covered

Your policy will be divided into categories of coverage, as will all insurance policies. Also listed will be exclusions in reference to some claims that may not be covered under that category of coverages. Here are just a few items which you will find in your policy:

STRUCTURAL COVERAGE

Your home and garage, even if they are not connected, are covered as well as other structures on the property listed as appurtenant, which could include a shed, barn, or pool. However, a structure used for business or rented to someone who is not a tenant is not covered, unless it is used as a private garage.

MINIMIZING DAMAGE

You must make every reasonable attempt to minimize the damage to your property before the company adjuster arrives. If you suffer damage from a fallen tree to your roof and the weather forecast calls for rain, you must attempt to prevent further damage.

Contact your agent and advise him/her of the damage. The insurance carrier will then be contacted and will send an adjuster as soon as possible. Unless the adjuster can get there the same day, notify the agent that you plan emergency repairs. In fact, get the good old camera out again, secure some photographs, and call a contractor to make the repairs as soon as possible.

You can clear the room of furniture or other objects that could become damaged. If there is damage to your carpets as a result of water from a frozen pipe that burst or rain entering the home, remove the water and get the items cleaned to save them. In fact, the insurance company could reimburse you for your time, possibly allowing hourly rates comparable to other laborers—it should be thankful that you took the time to minimize the damage.

REPAIR ESTIMATES

Secure estimates for any work to be done even if the adjuster is writing his/her own estimate. Once you settle with the company, you will then proceed to have the work done. Follow the same procedure as you would in an automobile claim. Have the contractor write up an estimate of damages. The insurance company and the contractor will then reach an agreed price, and you will receive the money less the deductible.

Chapter 11

Points of Interest in Your Policy

The following are some items in the basic homeowner's policy that you should be aware of.

Police Notification

You must always notify the police of any theft, burglary, or vandalism loss immediately upon the discovery of the crime. I mentioned this in the last chapter, and I will expound on this further. Claims can be questioned and even denied by your carrier if you do not report it. Also, it is a good idea to notify the police of any incident in which injury was involved if there is a possibility of a civil/criminal charge being filed by or against you or anyone insured under your policy.

This can apply whether the act occurred on or off the premises. I use the example in which your child strikes another child say with a stone, and injury results. This can be submitted under your homeowner's policy, if it is serious enough. By that I mean damage to the eye, scarring, etc. If your child is on his/her bicycle and injured in an accident with a vehicle or nonvehicle, it should be submitted.

These types of incidents could lead to a situation in which a report with the police would be filed. Also, if your dog should attack and bite someone, the injured party may and probably will file a report with the police and animal officer. It does not matter if your dog was restrained or not.

Injuries

Any person who is injured in a covered loss could have his/her medical expenses paid under the "medical payments" portion of your policy. The amount of coverage will be listed on your Declarations page. It could be for $1,000, $2,000, or $5,000. You must have whatever the minimum amount is, and the maximum the amount can be determined through you and your agent. Always carry more than necessary to be safe.

The money under this category pays for medical expenses only. If someone is making a claim against you above and beyond this, then the claim would be handled under the "liability" portion of your policy. This would apply to any incident on or off the premises, as long as the incident is a covered risk.

Claim vs. Suit

There may be times when a claim or suit is filed against you, and these are two different actions. Many people that I have dealt with on claims say that the person is "suing" them when in actuality the person has made a "claim" against them. First, the claim or incident has to exist. Then if there is no settlement made, the attorney for the party will file suit. To do this, he/she has a sheriff or constable issue a "summons and complaint" to you.

It is possible to be sued without a claim being filed. Then the summons and complaint would act as the notice that a claim has been filed. Upon receiving the summons and complaint, *immediately* turn it over to your carrier. If you have to submit it to your agent first, do so. The agent will mail it to the carrier. You may want to make a copy for your agent and personally deliver it to your carrier (if possible). Upon receipt of the notification, your carrier can verify the existence of the policy and coverage and commence the investigation with a statement from you. Just be sure that you have the right carrier with the right policy, and don't confuse the companies. This could lead to delays, and for this reason, the carrier usually advises the policyholder to submit the notice to the agent who can make the verification. If the agent can, and if your carrier is close by, perhaps you can then deliver the notice in person.

If and when suit is filled, don't panic and think that you are going to lose everything—even if the figure stated in the notice seeks $500,000 and you have only $100,000 on your policy.

The first order of business is to get the notice to your carrier. It will contact the attorney and advise him/her of the receipt or send the notice to an attorney representing you and your carrier to file an appearance, so that the suit is not lost by default. If the amount is within the coverage you have, then let your carrier handle the matter. If the amount is above your coverage, notify your attorney as well. He/she can then make an appearance on your behalf and seek to protect your assets. If no figure has been submitted, then the insurance company will determine it from the other attorney representing the "plaintiff." You are known as the "defendant," defending your position.

Again, once the figure is ascertained, the carrier will advise you of the amount, especially if it is over your policy limit. You then contact your attorney, who will follow the proceedings and keep you posted. If you have assets worthy of seeking or own a business, for example, the plaintiff attorney could seek money from you, *if the suit settles over the policy limits of your coverage.*

An example would be if the limits of coverage are $100,000 and the suit settles for $150,000. The attorney would conduct an assets check on you and see if it is worthwhile to seek the additional $50,000. If his/her client also has insurance coverage, then the attorney may (and generally does) pursue the action against the client's carrier. It is much easier to secure money from an insurance company than an individual if the suit warrants that amount.

Upon any payment, that carrier could subrogate against you for reimbursement to it. This is why the release might contain only your insurance company's name and not yours, as I mentioned in an earlier chapter. If your name is on the release, then the chances of going after you and collecting have been lost. If you are named in a suit and decide to switch the names of ownership of your property, check the laws in your state, as the change may not be recognized in a court of law.

Property Loss

In the event of a property loss, the carrier will send an adjuster or representative to assess the damage. It may sometimes use an expert to do this, possibly a contractor or independent with prior contractor experience. The carrier does not have someone perform the repairs, and this is why you seek your own contractor and assessment of damages. Carriers can be held responsible for any damage or unacceptable work its representatives might do if they did the job. And it is not good professional ethics for a contractor representing the insurance company to do the job.

When dealing with the company adjuster, keep in mind that he/she could be somewhat unaware of all the work necessary to complete the repairs. An adjuster who handles other types of claims as well as property is in a tough position to be fully aware of the current prices of items and sometimes the work involved. In fact, whatever the amount of work involved, you should be familiar with it as well. That is not to say that you have to do the work yourself. You still may have to get a contractor in your home as soon as possible, and you want to be involved in what is being done.

It is the policy of some carriers not to pay for part of the repairs until the work has been completed; this would depend on the type of policy in effect, the amount of coverage, and the value of your property. If you intend on doing the work yourself, the labor rate will vary, and unless you can show that this is your line of work, you could be paid at a rate less than contractor's price.

Deductible

Probably one of the most dreaded words in the insurance policy is "deductible." Everyone would like to receive the full amount on any loss, but, unfortunately, the deductible is part of the contract.

Don't forget that the deductible will apply to any claim you have against your company, including damage to your home or damage or theft to your personal property. Note too that the deductible is different for each type of loss. On theft losses, the deductible is generally $250, whereas on other losses it could be $100, $200, or $500. The Declarations page previously referred to will list not only your amounts of coverage, but also the deductible amount.

Like the deductible on your automobile policy, the homeowner's deductible or tenant's deductible amount depends on how much you are willing to pay on your premium. Some premiums allow a savings if the deductible is higher, but be prepared to absorb the amount when you have a claim. The amount will have to be determined by you and your agent, dependent on the property involved and your financial situation.

I cannot stress enough the importance of comparison shopping for insurance agents and policies. Get yourself the most affordable quality service and coverage you can.

Chapter 12

Workers' Compensation

In most states, a work-related injury falls under the category of "Workers' Compensation." In one state, possibly more, it can be referred to as "Industrial Accident." Whatever the terminology, it still refers to an accident that occurred at or during the course of your employment. All you really need to understand is that if you should sustain an injury which you and your treating physician feel is related to an activity that you performed on the job, then you would be entitled to benefits.

Medical Expenses/Substitution for Pay

You are entitled to any and all medical expenses for that particular injury, as well as the payments of benefits which substitute for your pay. Normally, this particular type of benefit is paid weekly, but it is not unusual to be paid biweekly, depending on the circumstances.

Scarring/Permanent Injury

You are also entitled to payment for any scarring and/or permanent injury above and beyond the medical and weekly benefits that you may receive. To make sure that you are being treated fairly, if you do not choose legal representation, contact your state Department of Workers' Compensation.

Reporting the Accident

If you have been involved in some type of work-related accident, then your employer will file a report after the incident is reported to him/her. You must report the accident to your employer, and the best time is right after it has occurred. I direct this to those people who may injure themselves but choose to overlook the injury or feel it too minor to report. If some time should pass before you report the accident, you could be in for a delay in receiving any benefits while the carrier investigates. Some people will report a work-related injury two or three weeks after it happened. That is quite a while for it to be reported. The carrier will surely investigate to make sure the injury did not occur outside of work.

Verification of Incident

If the case is to be investigated, then you will be asked to give a statement about the circumstances, sign a medical authorization, and submit any medical expenses that you have to the carrier. The carrier will verify the incident with your employer and any witnesses. It is important that you identify any witnesses. You may be working at a job in which you are the only employee from your company.

Secure the names of any witnesses along with the name of that person's employer, in case contact is to be made in the future. Cooperate with the carrier and understand that the investigation is conducted to protect not only the employer but also the employee, YOU.

Acceptance of Claim

If the claim is accepted, it will be recorded with the state department, and this assures that any future problems stemming from this accident will allow future payments to be made in a timely manner. In fact, this is where most of the problems with work-related claims arise. Sometimes the carrier is too slow in deciding if the claim is work-related or not. Consequently, the benefits are delayed and the person seeks legal counsel. In most cases (and I am citing a very high percentage), the carrier will end up paying benefits. Unfortunately, the attorney is already on the scene and the carrier has lost control of the injured party or claimant. Then the carrier cites the high cost of these claims and seeks an increase in the premiums the employers pay. This adds to an already volatile situation between the carrier and employer—all due to a slow process and lack of initiative to make a decision, accept a claim, and work with the injured person to return him/her to work.

Payment of Medical Bills

When the claim has been approved, the carrier will commence payment of all medical bills. You do not have to pay for your treatment. Don't forget to inform the treating hospital and/or doctor that the injury is work-related, and if you have the name of the carrier, give it to them. Doctors sometimes expect delays in payments, and since they are not in the collection agency business, they may ask for payment of their services up front. If this is the case, you may have to pay the bill. However, your payment will be reflected when the doctor sends a bill to the carrier. You should secure a receipt anyway for your records and present it when the time comes. In fact, keep all receipts and submit, no matter how small. Even if you have a receipt for sixty-nine cents, submit it. As I discussed in the automobile section of this book, you want to show the carrier what is essential in your treatment toward recovery. Besides, money is money, and the expense did come out of your pocket.

The carrier will pay all bills until you have been officially discharged by your doctor. If no further treatment is needed, then obviously there will be no more bills to pay. If, however, you are advised to return to work and see the doctor in three months or whatever time he/she suggests, the carrier has to honor that bill as well and any future bills. As long as the treatment is related to the incident and injury in question, the carrier must pay for it.

Lost Wages

Concerning your wages, the carrier will secure gross weekly earnings for a specific number of weeks prior to the week of incapacity from your employer. In other words, the carrier cannot include the week you injured yourself and started losing time from work. It would be like penalizing you, and it would reduce your compensation rate. Each state is different in the number of weeks used. The state in which I reside uses thirteen weeks, but some use fifty-two weeks. Whatever the amount, it is stated by law what is to be used. Once the carrier receives the earnings, it divides the total gross earnings by the number of weeks, which gives it the average weekly wage. Then the carrier takes a percentage of this, sometimes 66⅔ percent, sometimes 70 percent (again, whatever the state dictates), and this figure gives it the compensation rate.

Be aware that there is a maximum amount that the carrier is obligated to pay under state law. For instance, if you are on salary and gross $600 a week, and the percentage applied is 66⅔ percent, this would compute to $400 a week. The maximum amount for your state may be $350, so you would be eligible for only $350. The carrier would also add a specific amount for any dependents, if this is covered in your state. Using my state as an example, say a person is on a salary of $400 a week; $400 times 13 weeks (the number used in my state) equals $5,200. This figure divided by 13 equals $400. Taking 66⅔ percent of this figure equates to $264.92. Say the maximum in my state at this time is $360, the person receives $264.92 a week. If the person has two children under the age of eighteen and a wife who is unemployed, this state allows $9 for each dependent, for a total of $27. The total amount would then be $291.92. As long as this figure is not more than 80 percent of the person's average weekly wage, this figure is allowable. Again, remember each state is different in how the compensation rate is computed. Just ask to have it explained to you by the adjuster; in fact, demand it as your right.

If you were working two jobs at the time and are losing time from both, then the carrier includes the wages from both jobs to determine your rate. Thankfully, because of state laws, the carrier submits all of this information to the state and it is reviewed for approval, thereby protecting you.

Third Party Claims

If you are injured on the job and it is due to the negligence of another employer or your employer, you could have the right to pursue a liability claim. Under Workers' Compensation, pain and suffering is not included. However, by pursuing a "third party" claim against the negligent party, you could recover for pain and suffering. Two examples come to mind. One, you are working at a construction site and one of the other subcontractors fails to warn you about the temporary steps. You use the steps and fall through, injuring your back and leg. You could be entitled to Workers' Compensation and an action against the subcontractor's carrier.

In my second example, your employer puts you in a situation in which you are working in an inherently dangerous location, say on a staging or ladder that your employer owns and maintains. The employer knows the ladder is unsafe but allows you to work on it, and you injure yourself. You could have an action against your employer.

If it can be proven that another company caused your injury, then the carrier paying you benefits can subrogate or seek reimbursement from that company or its liability carrier. Then the carrier paying you benefits can receive all the money it paid out to you from the other carrier. You may engage the services of an attorney who could represent the carrier paying you benefits. He/she would protect the interest of that carrier, but also seek the additional money owed to you. You may or may not need legal representation. If you work with the carrier in its subrogation attempts against the other carrier, that carrier would deal with you directly. The seriousness of the injury may determine if you retain an attorney.

Settlement

Finally, in Workers' Compensation, you do not sign a release as you would in a liability claim. In some states your claim remains on record longer than the normal statute of say three years in a liability case. However, when you settle for scarring and/or loss of function or permanency, you will then release the carrier from further action on this portion of the claim. The carrier will notify the department of the settlement. In some states, the department must approve the settlement first. When agreement has been reached and you have been paid, then this concludes this portion of your claim. Your claim for medical bills and compensation remains open on record.

If, however, you are unable to return to your present position because of the injury or the carrier feels it is cost-effective to settle with you instead of continually paying you benefits for who knows how long, the carrier will pursue settlement. Here is when the case, if agreed upon, and usually with an attorney representing the claimant, is settled. At that time, the person can no longer make claim against that carrier. Your doctor will advise if you are unable to return to that occupation, and if the carrier's doctor concurs, then the alternative is settlement. It is then best to have legal representation.

Helpful Hints

Finally, here are just a few helpful hints on how to protect your rights and ensure a timely payment if you are injured at work.

Timely Reporting of Incident

No matter how minor the injury, make sure that you report it right away to your immediate supervisor. The injury could be only a small cut, but could develop into an infection and lead to lost time or further medical treatment. If something should occur later on and the matter was reported right away, the carrier would have little to dispute. All too often, a claim is questioned, delayed for payment, or controverted (denied) because the employer or the carrier questioned the time factor when the claim was reported. Carriers are skeptical of a late report because it suggests the possibility that the incident occurred elsewhere and was not work-related.

Communicate with Employer/Carrier

If you do sustain an injury that needs medical attention and leads to lost time from work, keep in constant communication with your employer and its carrier. First, you want your employer to be aware at all times of how you are progressing in your rehabilitation. Also, show it that you have every intention of returning to your job once the treating physician discharges you. Second, the carrier will consider it less likely that you are malingering or "milking" your injury. By maintaining this contact, you also keep current with the benefits being paid to you and the medical bills that should be getting paid. This avoids nasty telephone calls and repetitive bills that will be directed toward you if the bills aren't being paid.

Receipts

Keep all receipts of those bills that you have paid. These can include prescriptions, crutches, collars, foot pads, doctor and hospital bills, physical therapy, or whatever. For any bills that you receive that you have not paid, make a notation or a copy, and forward them to the carrier. Make sure to identify the bills by noting your claim number and the adjuster's name to prevent lost mail.

Physician

Have a good, reliable physician. All too often an injured person does not have a personal physician and does not know whom to contact. If you do not have a physician, check around and find one. It is also a good idea to have yearly checkups. Your physician can refer you to a specialist if you should ever need one. Likewise, if you do have your own doctor, then it makes it a little easier when you have to seek out a specialist and you would feel more comfortable, I'm sure.

Under Workers' Compensation, you can seek a second opinion at any time. This will be covered by the carrier, and it would depend on your injury and the results you are receiving if you decide to do this. Just advise the carrier whom you will be seeing so that it can request the report and bill.

Impartial/Independent Medical Examination

In reference to the above, the carrier could schedule you for an "impartial" or "independent" examination. This is when it schedules the appointment and pays for the service. You can, of course, reschedule if necessary. This gives the carrier confirmation of your injury and length of treatment needed, as well as determining if you are able to return to work. There are times when the "impartial" physician will advise the carrier that the person can return to work. If your own doctor agrees, then you would be obligated to return. If your doctor disagrees, however, then the carrier would file for a hearing.

Normally, the hearing rules in favor of the injured if the doctor's report specifies more treatment is needed. If both doctors feel that you can return back to work on a limited basis, then you would be obligated to try it. If it does not work, then your doctor would state this and resumption of benefits would commence. If you are able to work on a part-time basis, the carrier has to make up the difference between what you now gross and your previous gross weekly earnings. For example, suppose your weekly earnings before the accident were $500, and now working only twenty hours per week, you gross $250. In my state, the carrier pays 66⅔ percent of the difference (66⅔ percent of $250) or $165.58, which you receive with the $250 for a total of $415.58. This is an incentive to resume full-time work and puts you in the area you were making prior to the accident, less taxes. This may differ from state to state, but it is an entitlement to you if you return to work on a limited basis.

Unaccepted Claims

If your claim is not accepted by the carrier, your options are to accept or appeal that decision. It would be best to retain legal counsel if the claim is controverted (denied). If there is a fee by the attorney, it would normally be paid by the carrier if the case is won. There are some hearings, called informal hearings, in which no fee is required. Also, in some states the attorney is not paid unless the case is settled completely. Check your state's code if you are unsure.

Residing in a Different State than You Work

If you reside in one state but were hired in another, you may be able to choose the benefits from either state. It may be that one state has a higher maximum rate than the other, which would mean more money if your salary dictates this. However, the medical expenses are always paid 100 percent by the carrier.

If you deal with the carrier by yourself, you may be asked to give a statement, either recorded or written. You will also be asked to sign a medical authorization and other forms necessary to process your claim. The forms generally used are the wage form listing your earnings, an agreement that the carrier has accepted your claim, and in states where applicable, a dependency status form, listing dependents such as your wife and children under eighteen living and not living with you.

Once you are able to return to work, you may have to sign an agreement that states the carrier does not pay you anymore since you are receiving your usual wages. Understand that this form also mentions that by signing it, you do not give up your rights for benefits in the future if you are entitled. All these forms are sent to the department for its records to make the department aware of your claim and its status. If you have any questions about any forms, do not hesitate to contact the carrier for an explanation, which it should graciously give.

Statement to Carrier

In reference to the statement that you give to the carrier, it should be as factual as possible. The adjuster has a list of questions that will be asked, whether the statement is recorded or written. I have included in this book a statement for an automobile claim. The basics for the Workers'

Compensation claim are the same. The following information should be emphasized:

1. Full name and present address; future address if applicable so that you get your benefits
2. Age, social security number, marital status, and children
3. Employment history, usually within a ten-year period
4. Previous injuries and the specifics
5. Facts of the accident
6. Places of treatment
7. Out-of-pocket expenses
8. Representation by an attorney

If you had injured the same area previously, the carrier will investigate and may wish to secure the medical records for those injuries. There are a couple of reasons for this. First, the aggravation of a previous injury, although considered a new injury if there is a new incident, can be accepted by the carrier. The information does give the carrier an idea of how long it will take you to return to work. Second, if the previous injury, again to the same area, were also related, the carrier could seek reimbursement for what it pays out under a fund set up by the state. It does not affect your claim. If, however, you injured yourself at work and never completely recovered and/or continued to be treated and the carrier then is different from the one presently handling your claim, a delay could arise. The present carrier, in an attempt to get the previous carrier to pay benefits, could controvert your claim to force a hearing. You will be paid regardless—it just causes a delay.

This is an isolated incident and may not apply to you. However, you should understand the carrier's position and the types of claims that it deals with. Most of the claims are legitimate and easy to approve. The only way to do this, however, is to investigate and secure as much information as you can give. If you are faced with a situation in which benefits are not being paid, and it is out of your control, perhaps you can apply for some other benefits in the meantime. Then that agency can file a lien on what was paid and that should hold you until the matter is resolved. Check with your local Department of Labor. In my area I know of "Temporary Disability Insurance," and welfare assistance.

Retaining the Services of a Lawyer

On whether to retain the services of a lawyer, I would advise that you cooperate with the carrier, give it as much information as you can, and await its decision. If your claim is controverted, then seek legal counsel.

You could retain counsel at the beginning of your claim, but the carrier will still have to investigate and a hearing may be filed, which could take a month to hear. Besides, the carrier may feel your claim is questionable if you have an attorney immediately, and your main concern should be prompt payment of benefits.

If the injury is serious or if death results, then I suggest an attorney be called. The situation is too traumatic to handle alone, and the attorney will make sure that you or your beneficiaries receive what is entitled to you and to them.

Medical Authorization

The medical authorization is needed in some states to secure your medical records. The adjuster may request that you sign one, and doing so will avoid delays if it is needed by some doctor or hospital before they will release the information. Medical bills are generally releasable without the authorization, but it is the reports that are more important to the carrier. The reports will document the facts of the accident and also show any previous injury. They will also show any evidence of alcohol or drugs, if tests were done for these.

The authorization is just that—it is not a release and should specify that it is not. Also, make sure the authorization is completed *before* you sign it. It has been a common practice for adjusters to secure a blank authorization if they wanted to use it to secure medical information in regard to another incident. It must specify the date of the accident it is being used for. Once your claim has been closed, the authorization can never be used for any purpose. You will also sign an authorization if you were treated at a hospital, and this allows the hospital only to release information. The authorization you sign for the carrier allows the hospital to release the information to it. This security came about with the advent of the Privacy Act, which prevents information from being released to anyone without the person's authorization.

Wage Authorization

In some instances, you will also be asked to sign a "wage authorization," which allows your employer to release information about your wages to the carrier. This is normally used by independents, as the carriers can get this information directly since they insure your employer. The authorization can also be used to secure information from your previous employer(s), so read it carefully and decide if you wish to allow this.

Filing for a Hearing

The next topic of discussion is the hearing. If the carrier controverts your claim and you accept the decision, then you receive no benefits. If you feel you are entitled to these benefits, then you will have to file for a hearing. You will be contacted by the department that your claim has been controverted. You can, at that time, ask if your state requires an attorney to represent you. I think that it is a good idea to hire one anyway. The attorney will file for a hearing date, at which time arguments will be heard from both sides.

The main facts you have to show at a hearing are that you suffered an injury at work, reported it within a reasonable amount of time, and received medical treatment. With that information, it will be tough for the carrier to show why it refused to accept your claim. Again, I am referring to a legitimate claim, and if it is one, you should not even reach the stage of a hearing, unless, of course, the carrier does not have a medical report. Keep in mind that in some states, unless you are receiving benefits, you do not have to attend an "impartial" examination. If one is scheduled and you have nothing to hide, then attend. Ask the carrier if this is so, and to confirm it, check with the Workers' Compensation Department.

If for some reason you lose at the hearing, your attorney can appeal. Again, you decide how much you want to pursue this, but if you feel that you are entitled, then do so.

Activity Check

Carriers routinely use the services of independent investigators to conduct activity checks, background checks, and surveillance, so don't be alarmed if you should find yourself in this situation.

In an activity check, the investigator questions your neighbors about your activities to determine if you are working while you are on disability. In the background check, your records at the town/city hall and other sources are examined to see if you have had previous claims. Surveillance is sometimes set up to follow you to see if you show any signs of injury or are working somewhere when you should not be. This information can be introduced at a hearing.

So if you are disabled and receiving benefits, don't take the chance of being caught. Follow your doctor's instructions, and pursue a hobby or read if you have to keep active. Clear it with your doctor first, and if he/she agrees, then you can start doing some activities. You can also go on vacation, even if you are collecting benefits. As long as the doctor feels that the rest will be good for you, if you plan to be in perhaps Florida for a month, you should be able to make arrangements with the carrier to have your money forwarded to you during your stay. I would think that as long as the location is within a reasonable distance, it should not refuse. You can even be checked out by a doctor where you are staying, and the carrier should pay the bill. After all, you are still maintaining an interest in your health.

The bottom line is to report the incident on a timely basis, seek medical treatment, even as a precautionary measure, and maintain contact with your employer and carrier, and especially advise them when you are able to return to work. Also, keep all records and receipts and cooperate with the employer and carrier so your claim will be handled more smoothly, benefits get paid timely, and you can concentrate on getting better.

Chapter 13

Alternatives if Your Claim Is Not Paid

You have submitted a claim to the carrier and received written notice that your claim has been denied. If the claim pertains to Workers' Compensation, it is referred to as being "controverted." What do you do if you feel that you are entitled to benefits?

Workers' Compensation

Assuming your claim is work-related, you will need to first contact the carrier to determine why the controversion took place. When the carrier refuses to pay benefits (this would include medical bills as well), the carrier must notify the state department that handles Workers' Compensation filings. The department can be referred to as the Department of Workers' Compensation, the usual name, or in a state such as Massachusetts, the Industrial Accident Board. Determining the correct name is just a matter of checking the telephone book for state listings, or ask your employer.

That department, when notified, will in turn contact you and advise you of the controversion and the reason.

89

You can then contact the carrier to see if there is anything you can do to change its mind or secure a report or document that it may not have received. If the matter is still to be controverted, secure the services of an attorney. I recommend this whether your state stipulates it or not. If you are still out of work, see if your state has temporary disability benefits, which may pay you in the meantime. If you do receive this type of benefit, that agency will simply file a lien against the carrier if you are awarded benefits in the future. This award will either be because the carrier received the information it needed to make a decision, or a hearing was held upon request by your attorney. The bottom line is that if you and your treating physician feel that the injury you have sustained is work-related, then you should fight for the benefits, and you should win.

Automobile Accident

If the claim pertains to an automobile accident and payment is being denied because the carrier feels that you were the sole or major contributor to the accident (depending on how the law reads in your state), then seek legal counsel. You can again contact the carrier to see why the denial was made and if you can rectify the opinion of the carrier. Sometimes a mutual agreement can be reached between you and the carrier. However, it is unlikely that you will be paid the full amount, as it would have offered it to you in the first place. If you are comfortable with a lesser amount, then you decide. If you feel you should receive the full amount you seek, then see an attorney. Let the attorney review the accident and advise you. You have to understand that the carrier is a larger and more financially secure entity than you. So it is not easily threatened by a lawyer. Sometimes it would just as soon deal with an attorney than you. Plus, it figures it has the money and you don't, so if you intend to fight, it can outspend you. Or it figures you will just get fed up and take anything just to get out of this situation. This is why there are a few carriers with reputations for not paying anything. That is, of course, hyperboling, but they will not pay what one feels they should pay. So the claim goes into suit and what they end up paying out is the interest on what they felt the case was worth. This is called the "reserve."

Homeowner/Renting an Apartment/Owning a Business

If your claim involves your home, condominium, apartment, or business and you are denied or your claim value is reduced, ask why and get all the details. The adjuster has to take the time to explain this to you or you are being shortchanged in the contract. If the carrier refuses to budge and again you feel that you deserve more, have an attorney review the situation. Or you can hire a "public" adjuster to whom you give power of attorney, and the public adjuster deals with carrier. You yourself can request arbitration. To do this you first should file a "proof of loss," which is a form you obtain from the carrier documenting the amount that you feel your claim is worth. Again, I could be referring to a theft loss or property damage loss in which your figures don't match the adjuster's. Return the proof of loss, along with a request for arbitration. This is a right stated in your homeowner's policy.

Send the request certified or registered so it can be documented when the carrier received it.

Be advised that the carrier can request arbitration also, but it tends to be the policyholder. Each party then selects an appraiser, which you can find in the Yellow Pages or ask your agent. The identity of the appraisers must be made to each party within a number of days, normally twenty. Again, check your policy. The appraisers then select an umpire who is impartial and competent. If an umpire cannot be agreed upon within fifteen days, the matter can go before a judge of record in that particular state or jurisdiction.

The process sounds long and tedious, but compared to the time involved if suit is filed, this is not an unrealistic way of resolving the matter.

As I stated earlier, the public adjuster would be useful if the claim is substantial, too complex or time-consuming for you to document. Whereas an attorney will work on a percentage of the amount settled (usually one-third), the public adjuster usually works on a smaller percentage, like 10–20 percent—you will have to determine what the fee is. The public adjuster would be more experienced in these matters, handling them more often than an attorney might.

There are times when the carrier will try to push the matter into suit. The carrier may feel the chances are better in questioning the damages in this option rather than taking a chance with arbitration. The circumstances that I have been exposed to show that the policyholder is generally the one who files for either arbitration or suit. If you have to have your claim heard by either option, choose arbitration. If the carrier attempts to have the matter go into suit, again push or have your attorney let it be known that you prefer arbitration.

It is important that you work with the carrier, whether it be yours or the other party's. Supply it with as much information as you can. This is contrary to what some attorneys will tell you. My feeling is if you have a legitimate claim and nothing to hide, then why not? The carrier is only trying to ascertain the facts and what is pertinent to the case so it can evaluate it objectively and fairly. This is how the system should operate. Unfortunately, it sometimes does not and the stigma that carriers are not to be trusted and will take advantage of people remains. This usually involves an inexperienced adjuster and policyholder.

When you deal with a carrier, know your facts and be patient within a reasonable time. Accept what you feel is fair and in line with what facts have been reported to the carrier. It would be nice if the carrier could use a lie detector or crystal ball to see who is telling the truth and who is stretching it. How easy this job would be then!

A Personal Experience

Let me share an experience with you which I had with an insurance company concerning a claim.

A short time ago, specifically in October 1988, my wife was involved in an automobile accident. She was operating my vehicle, which was uninsured at the time. I was seeking coverage at the time and, as luck would have it, the accident occurred. Luckily, there were no injuries. However, both vehicles were moved after the fact and my wife failed to seek out witnesses.

The police report was not a factor in determining liability, as they took no statements from either operator. The facts of the accident were as follows:

The accident took place on a four-lane road, two lanes in each direction. My wife was emerging from a hamburger establishment and wanted to turn right onto the inner lane of this road. She observed traffic to her left and saw vehicles approaching in the outer lane only. Her lane was clear. None of the approaching vehicles had a turn signal operating to signify a lane change into the inner lane. With the lane clear, my wife pulled out and claims to have been 99 percent into the inner lane. As she is not one to exaggerate or lie, I believe her story.

Suddenly, one of the vehicles entered her lane and

the collision ensued. Damage to my vehicle was to the left front corner. Damage to the other vehicle was to the passenger door. The owner of the other vehicle collected under her collision carrier. The carrier then subrogated against me for the entire amount, deductible included.

I took a statement from my wife and submitted it to the other operator's carrier, along with a diagram of the accident. I wrote it a letter explaining our point of view. Now keep in mind that the accident occurred in October 1988. First contact of any kind from the adverse carrier was in February 1989. Never once did the carrier contact my wife or me to discuss the claim, the property damage, or to determine if there were any injuries. The company's office in my state simply paid its insured and sent the file to its subrogation department, which is located in another state.

The letter of subrogation I received requested that I pay the carrier the specified amount. Since I am in the business and since I was curious to see how this would be handled, I waited for the carrier to contact me. After receiving my report, the carrier reduced the amount it had sought from 100 percent to 80 percent. Since the carrier now saw liability on its operator, I submitted a claim for the damage to my car. I secured two estimates from reputable auto body shops, demanding an estimate written accurately. I was now dealing with the local claim office and it did not want my estimates. It stated that it would send an appraiser, which it did. I never received a copy of the appraisal, nor an amount they wrote. My main objective was to reduce it even more, seeing that the carrier was admitting liability in part on their insured, and in my state the percentage of liability is used to determine what you receive from the other carrier.

My car was driveable, although the damage was not worth repairing, so I was not concerned about being paid; I was merely concerned with reducing what I would have to pay out. I had already surmised and confirmed that if the matter went into suit, the court would find the parties at fifty-fifty liability.

Now comes the fun part! The claim office wrote me a letter denying liability on their insured and offered me no payment. Since their subrogation office was seeking 80 percent, by law I would be entitled to 20 percent which I felt was still unacceptable. I wrote to the claim office explaining this and offered the following: If they would accept 50 percent liability from me, I would waive the damage to my vehicle. The subrogation office wrote back saying that the 80 percent they sought was more than fair and they would put matters into the hands of their lawyers.

I first received notice from the lawyer in August of 1989. I contacted the lawyer and explained the entire events of the accident. I also reconfirmed my offer. The attorney accepted. I asked him why the carrier did not make this decision months ago when I first proposed it, and he stated that it was company procedure to send the file to an attorney if agreement could not be reached.

I should add that I now have coverage on my vehicle, although I thought I handled it better alone. I'm afraid that if I had been insured, the amount of 80 percent may have been paid just to close the claim. Coverage is still necessary, though, and I was lucky.

My purpose in relating this story is to give you an example of how an insurance company can handle a claim. It will be different from claim to claim, of course, but by documenting my claim, based solely on the truth, and remaining firm in my convictions, I attained my goal. Despite the fact that the carrier was given different theories of liability, it never contacted my wife or me to discuss the claim, and could not make a decision within a reasonable time period. The claim could have settled much sooner and needless legal expense could have been avoided. Unless, of course, its legal counsel is on a retainer fee. Then the carrier is unconcerned.

Glossary

Adjuster—A person who can work directly for the carrier or independently; has the responsibility to investigate a claim and determine liability. If damage is within authority, the adjuster can settle directly. If not within authority, the adjuster has to seek it from superior.

Appraiser—A person who can work for the carrier directly or as an independent. Main duties are to inspect and determine the extent and cost to repair automobile damage. In some cases, an appraiser can take statements, determine liability, and settle a claim on the spot.

Carrier—Referred to as the insurance company.

Claim—This is what you submit to an insurance company when you either cause damage or injury or suffer damage or injury.

Claimant—Anyone making a claim against the insurance company.

Controvert—Refers to a work-related injury and the denial of benefits to that party making a claim for benefits.

Documentation—The key to the successful handling and completion of any claim. Keep records, receipts, proofs of existence, paid bills, estimates, and anything pertaining to your claim. Also document facts about the claim you can recount in chronological order. Let the insurance company tell you what is and is not covered and why.

Insured—Refers to the policyholder or anyone covered under that policy.

Insurer—Also referred to as the insurance company.

Investigator—A person who simply obtains the facts and reports back to the carrier (whereas an adjuster handles the claim in its entirety toward a conclusion).

Medical Authorization—When injuries are involved, this is signed by the claimant. It is necessary that the insurance company have this if it is to obtain your medical records. It allows any doctor, hospital, or other facility of treatment to release your medical records to the company requesting same. It should release only those records pertaining to the current injury. In order for prior information to be released, it will have to be stipulated on the authorization as well.

Physical Damage—Refers to damage sustained by an automobile, truck, motorcycle, etc.

Proof of Loss—This is used in place of a release on claims for automobile, home, and personal property damage. It is signed by the insured and identifies the amount of the claim and the settlement figure.

Property Damage—Normally refers to a homeowner's claim and damage sustained to your home. Some carriers will also refer to your automobile damage as property damage.

Release—A form an individual signs after settling a claim with the insurance company. It is normally binding; the signer gives up the right to pursue future action against that insurance company.

Statement—A description of the facts pertaining to any claim, when applicable. The three common methods of statements are: (1) company form, (2) recorded, or (3) written. You should have a copy of your statement no matter which procedure is used. (The recorded statement can be done in person or on the telephone, and you would want to request a copy of it once transcribed.)

Subrogation—When an insurance company pays out any money to its insured and seeks restitution from another party for reimbursement.

Suit—A claim is in suit only when you have been issued a summons and complaint or when one has been filed on your behalf.

Wage authorization—This allows the release of your wages from your employer. It can also release your application or work file, but it should only pertain to your wages. Again, the authorization could release, if signed, a previous employment history, and you should be aware of this.

The words above are just some of those commonly used and misused by people I have encountered. Understand and question any words used by the insurance company that you do not understand. For people to believe that they are being "sued," when in fact they only have a claim against them, can be an uneasy feeling.